UNMUSICAL NEW YORK

Da Capo Press Music Reprint Series

MUSIC EDITOR
BEA FRIEDLAND
Ph.D., City University of New York

UNMUSICAL NEW YORK

A BRIEF CRITICISM OF
TRIUMPHS, FAILURES, & ABUSES

By HERMANN KLEIN
WITH A PORTRAIT OF THE AUTHOR

DA CAPO PRESS • NEW YORK • 1979

Library of Congress Cataloging in Publication Data

Klein, Hermann, 1856-1934.
   Unmusical New York.

   (Da Capo Press music reprint series)
   Reprint of the 1910 ed. published by J. Lane,
London, New York.
   1. Music—New York (City) I. Title.
ML200.8.N5K5   1979   780'.9747'1   79-1278
   ISBN 0-306-79517-5

2 2 6 2 0 6

This Da Capo Press edition of *Unmusical New York:
A Brief Criticism of Triumphs, Failures, and Abuses*
is an unabridged republication of the first edition
published in New York and London in 1910 by
John Lane Company and The Bodley Head Ltd.

Published by Da Capo Press, Inc.
A Subsidiary of Plenum Publishing Corporation
227 West 17th Street, New York, N.Y. 10011

UNMUSICAL NEW YORK

UNMUSICAL NEW YORK

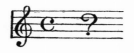

A BRIEF CRITICISM OF
TRIUMPHS, FAILURES, & ABUSES
By HERMANN KLEIN
WITH A PORTRAIT OF THE AUTHOR

LONDON : JOHN LANE THE BODLEY HEAD
NEW YORK : JOHN LANE COMPANY MCMX

WILLIAM CLOWES AND SONS, LIMITED, LONDON AND BECCLES.

WITH A FIRM BELIEF IN
THE FUTURE OF AMERICAN MUSIC
I CORDIALLY DEDICATE THESE PAGES TO
THOSE EARNEST WORKERS WHO CONSTITUTE
THE RISING MUSICAL TALENT
OF THE UNITED STATES OF AMERICA

PREFACE

THIS book consists mainly of the text—revised and enlarged—of a lecture which I gave at Bechstein Hall, London, in October, 1909, under the title of "The Truth about Music in America." Let me confess that that title was somewhat misleading—unintentionally, of course. I should have used the word "New York," not "America." I had forgotten that names of places which convey the same idea to the English mind are far from being synonymous to the American.

Nor had I altogether intended the "truth" in this instance to be looked upon as a revelation of things concealed—of things mysteriously kept from the light of day; but rather as an *exposé* of musical conditions as I had studied them myself, and which, if familiar to the initiated, had not previously been described or put into concrete shape.

Thus the lecture had a curiously diverse effect. In London, where it was heard and criticized at first hand, it was declared to be much milder and less sensational than had been expected. In New York, thanks to the garbled reports sent to certain papers, it was represented as being a tissue of mis-statements and exaggerations. Consequently, it became doubly incumbent upon me to publish in book form my experiences and comments in connection with this subject.

I cannot hope that this volume will please every one. A literary effort which is a piece of candid criticism and advice rarely does, no matter how well meant, no matter how purely based upon honest opinion and actual fact. But I have, at least, sedulously striven to avoid giving offence ; and if I have not altogether succeeded, I shall be comforted by the reflection that I have performed a duty which I had no right to shirk. The impartial reader will judge whether I might have said or done less. Only an extremist will go so far as to argue that I ought to have said more.

One word in conclusion concerning the title of this book. Some may think it undeserved, others will not. Only those, however, who mistake the inner meaning of the word "musical," as applied to a city, will venture to declare that New York has arrived at the æsthetic stage where it can without question claim that adjective for its own. *Ergo*, if New York be not genuinely musical, what is it? Again the reader shall decide.

HERMANN KLEIN.

LONDON,
December 1909.

CONTENTS

		PAGE
	PREFACE	vii
I.	INTRODUCTORY : THE RÔLE OF THE CANDID FRIEND	3
II.	NEW YORK AS A MUSICAL CENTRE . .	8
III.	NEW YORK AMATEURS AND THE "STAR" SYSTEM	16
IV.	CONCERNING NEW YORK AUDIENCES . .	25
V.	HOW NATIVE TALENT IS TREATED . .	33
VI.	INSTITUTIONS AND THEIR EXPLOITERS . .	45
VII.	AUTOCRATS OF THE OPERA HOUSE :	
	MAURICE GRAU	53
	HEINRICH CONRIED	60
	OSCAR HAMMERSTEIN	65
	GATTI-CASAZZA AND DIPPEL . . .	75
VIII.	GENII OF THE CONCERT WORLD . . .	80
IX.	MUSIC IN THE CHURCHES	99
X.	THE COURSE OF MUSICAL CULTURE . .	107
XI.	MUSICAL CRITICISM : THE REAL AND THE IDEAL	122
	ENVOI	141

UNMUSICAL NEW YORK

UNMUSICAL NEW YORK

I.—INTRODUCTORY : THE RÔLE OF THE CANDID FRIEND

"TO see ourselves as others see us." A precious faculty, truly ; yet even harder for a community to acquire than an individual, and hardest of all, no doubt, for the vast group of communities which we call a country. Then how to make profitable use of the faculty, if actually it be ours ?

Let us consider the matter.

To one who has travelled much and dwelt in large cities nothing can be more striking that the gregarious quality which enables men and nations to lead their lives and conduct their own affairs in a manner peculiar to themselves. Their habits and customs are unlike their neighbours' ; they cultivate different ideas, different ideals ; they think and move in circles restricted to the boundaries of their local sphere of action ; they are, as a rule, supremely indifferent to external effect and the impression created upon the " foreigner."

America shares this human characteristic with the rest of the world. But there is one redeeming quality, not common to all, which the youngest of the great nations must be emphatically credited with, and that is a willingness to learn. Confess it or not, as he may, the American is ever ready to seize upon a weak spot and strengthen it. Let him once recognize that there is something in his commercial or artistic economy which he can improve, and he will at least make an effort to achieve the upward step.

Failing the introspective gift—the power to perceive our own shortcomings as others perceive them—there remains an alternative not quite so flattering to the national dignity, but perhaps in the end more conducive to accurate judgment and reliable consequences, namely, to

lend an attentive ear to the stranger who has
sojourned long enough within the gates to
become familiar with actual conditions, and is
sufficiently daring to play the part of the
"candid friend."

Dear reader, will you listen?

My theme is Music; and if you will but
"bid me discourse" (not in melody, but in
honest English prose), I will lay before you a
frank recital of facts and opinions concerning
one of the most complex situations that ever
confronted the musical inhabitants of a city
It may not precisely "enchant thine ear," but
I think it will divert and edify you—that is, if
you be at all interested in the inner working of
matters connected with the so-called "divine
art."

I have allotted to myself the rôle of the
"candid friend" in this instance because I
feel that I am the right person to play it. It
has not been forced upon me; neither have I
any deep-laid purpose to serve in undertaking
it. I simply know that there are things to say
which ought to be said. I shall say them,

moreover, with a full sense of the gratitude that I owe to the country in which I spent more than seven busy years of my life, meeting with much friendly sympathy, much cordial hospitality and kindness that I can never forget.

The rôle is a notoriously ungrateful one, of course ; but that does not signify so long as motives are not misunderstood or wilfully misinterpreted. Nor do I begin with any apology for speaking publicly and plainly upon a subject which I conceive to be of universal interest.

Before leaving England to live in New York, in December, 1901, I had worked as a musical journalist for five and twenty years, taking an active part in London musical life and keeping under constant observation the development of modern musical thought. It had been my intention to devote myself in America exclusively to teaching singing. As a matter of fact, by the time I went to reside in England once more, in June, 1909, I had performed in New York the triple functions of singing-teacher, musical critic, and concert-giver. I was best known in the first-named capacity ; the second and third I filled respectively during the opening and concluding years of my stay.

Once a critic, always a critic, I suppose. Even when not acting as a professional chronicler, I found recreation in attending all the more important operatic and concert performances. If I did not write, I took mental notes. In a word, I observed at close range what was going on in the musical world of New York.

It is the outcome of these observations that I propose to embody in the following pages. Even a retired critic occasionally feels an irresistible impulse to voice his conclusions, especially when he believes that in so doing he may achieve some slight service.

And now to really begin.

II.—NEW YORK AS A MUSICAL CENTRE

THIS is to be a study of Music in New York, not Music in America. Originally I intended it to be the latter, but soon I perceived that the subject was too vast to be adequately handled within the limits at my disposal.

Besides, the distinction between New York and other big American cities, adjacent or distant, is (as every true American knows) wide as the poles asunder. Nor is it less so in a musical sense than any other. Ask a cultured Bostonian or even a somnolent Philadelphian to tell you calmly and without prejudice whether he thinks the musical public of New York may be regarded as representative, in its tastes, its discernment and its judgment, of the musical public of the United States?

The answer will come swiftly, and in the negative.

Surely it is not mere jealousy that causes these worthy neighbours to take a pride in differentiating themselves and their opinions from the huge cosmopolis which occupies the Island of Manhattan.

As an Englishman I cannot be accused of partiality in this matter. Well, if you demand of me—Are the Boston audiences more genuinely musical ? are they better trained to understand and appreciate the fine points in an important work or a new artist or a high-class performance ? are they more difficult to satisfy, less fickle when they are satisfied ?—I reply unhesitatingly, Yes !

But, after all, it is not to these other cities, however much more purely American they may be, that European musical celebrities direct their preliminary steps. They land to-day, as they did all through the nineteenth century, at New York. If they be operatic singers, it is there that they find what was until recently their abiding-place and what is still their chief centre. If they be virtuosi of the piano or the violin, New York is still their main objective.

It is there, whether they would go farther afield or not, that tradition expects them to first submit themselves to the ordeal of critical opinion ; and *pace* Boston, I venture to assert that the verdict of New York will largely affect, if it does not actually decide one way or the other, the subsequent career of any artist in the United States. To New York, first of all, come the visiting composers, the " star " conductors, the English oratorio singers (what few there are now) ; and in that city are witnessed the *premières* of all the new operas, the first performances of most of the new orchestral and choral works.

There can be no doubt, I am convinced, that New York is the principal centre of musical life in America. On the other hand, apart from its position, its size, and its wealth, does it possess the true essentials—speaking from an artistic standpoint—for wielding the power that it claims as by right ?

With the attractive force of a loadstone, the

destructive weight of a Juggernaut, the enriching resources of King Solomon's Mines, New York in my opinion still lacks in a lamentable degree those highest qualities of taste and judgment which could alone render it worthy to fill the position among the musical capitals of the world to which it so eagerly aspires.

Before going further, it may be well to reflect for a moment upon the justice of a comment which has been made as to the similarity between musical conditions in New York and London.   I have not the least desire to shirk this question, since I hold no brief for one side or the other.

Only I am now dealing with New York. I have lived there long enough to know it thoroughly, and the moment seems to me to be timely for discussing its real musical status and the methods of those who pull its chief musical wires.

That London is guilty of similar sins and shortcomings may be perfectly true.   I have little doubt that it is.   Indeed, go where you

will, to Paris, Berlin, Vienna, or any of the
great European centres, you will find certain
features in the musical cosmos—certain peculiarities of indifference, of intolerance, of indis-
crimination and perhaps even harshness—that
are common to all.

But to allege that the conditions in these
various places are absolutely identical would
not be a greater error than to suppose that
ultra-modern New York is musically in the
same *galère* with London up-to-date, either for
precisely the same reasons or with precisely the
same results.   The results may bear a resem-
blance, as do earthly troubles of every kind in
every land ; but the reasons, I venture to argue,
present as many points of difference as do the
political and social customs of these two
gigantic, overgrown cities.

I prefer to leave, at any rate for a while, the
discussion of the delicate question, Which is
the less musical city of the two, London or
New York ? That does not actually enter into
the scope of my discourse. Perchance it may
be taken up one day by an American critic

who shall have lived as long in London as I
have in New York. Meanwhile the description,
faithfully set down, of musical conditions in
the latter place should suffice to establish the
nature of the distinction to which I have
referred. If so, it ought to have a usefulness
of its own on that account.

To European musicians New York and
America have much the same signification. If
the rest of the United States think otherwise I
can only say the mistake is liable to continue
so long as the Empire City occupies the
geographical and social position that it does.
It has even occurred that an artist who has
paid a brief visit to New York has gone away
in the solemn belief that nothing further was
necessary to obtain the *cachet* of an American
success.

Not long ago a well-known singer crossed
in a fast Cunarder, stayed a fortnight at a hotel
on Broadway, and returned home without
having sung a note. Shortly afterwards the
singer was announced to reappear at a concert

" after a brilliantly successful tour in America," and no doubt the fact was taken for granted without any question.

The same proceeding would scarcely be possible from the other side of the Atlantic, where they have a habit of asking for press notices—upon which, indeed, the European success of an American artist is largely dependent.

To the European artist New York remains as surely as it ever was the Mecca of the musical world, the city of huge fees and tempting salaries, where success can be rapidly achieved with the aid of a neatly-executed boom and an enterprising press-agent.

Well, the Mecca may still be on the map, but I am sorry for the majority of the sanguine pilgrims who journey thither with the idea of propitiating the Prophet by dint of assiduous worship at the shrine of the millionaires.

Truth to tell, the Mecca is nowadays little more than a myth of departed ages. Unless the artist be gifted in a very exceptional degree, he or she never gets within kneeling distance of the shrine. It may be possible to catch a glimpse of the outer walls ; but as for putting a foot inside the temple or coming to close quarters with the priestesses of the " Four Hundred "—no such luck !

III.—NEW YORK AMATEURS AND THE "STAR" SYSTEM

IN one sense amateurs of good music, the world over, are cast in much the same mould. Give them their money's worth in a form that pleases their fancy, and they will not only go away content, but, at reasonable intervals, extend you their patronage again and again.

In New York the hardest part of the problem lies in the query—how to catch your amateur the first time ?

This is a difficult business, for the reason that New York is absolutely spoiled. Like London, it is simply overladen with musical talent of every grade ; it is satiated by a constant succession of musical entertainments of every description. Why then should this public be expected to fling its dollars at an artist of unknown calibre or ordinary accomplishments more freely than Londoners will expend their half-guineas upon equally talented and equally unknown American performers?

The amateur who enjoys a social standing can only be captured by means of personal introduction; and woe betide the foreign musician who pays an initial visit to New York unarmed with this outward and visible emblem of the international *entente*! Even then, though, it will be found that a custom familiar enough in Europe prevails here also —the hostess who purchases tickets for the concert expects the artist to sing or play in her *salon* for nothing; which may or may not be considered by the impartial observer as a very fair *quid pro quo*.

Sometimes, however, the bargain is not struck beforehand and mistakes may occur. I remember hearing of a case in which the social function came after the concert, and the artist (a talented violinist), not receiving a cheque for giving what was practically a recital before a large party of guests, duly

c

sent in his bill. After a few days the cheque arrived ; but, needless to say, the lady was never "at home" to that violinist again, and she patronized his concerts no more.

Of course, the distinguished musician who ranks as a "star" comes under a different category. The services of a leading prima donna, or a great tenor, or a renowned instrumentalist must be sought and paid for, very often at fabulous prices.

Once a year the New York multi-millionairess takes infinite pride in giving her private concert, providing for the occasion a couple of stars and perhaps a small orchestra to fill in the background. It is not with her a question of economy. The flowers and the supper will cost thousands of dollars. But it is worthy of note that where the artists are concerned she expects one or two swallows to constitute her entire summer. Whether it is because she fears to upset her stars by engaging too large a constellation, or because she hesitates to spoi her friends by giving them too much, I am unable to say. The fact remains.

Except at the Opera, what are termed "combination casts" do not seem to find favour in New York, where individual stars are simply adored. I did not know this before I went there, but I was destined to quickly find it out.

In the spring of 1902, shortly after my arrival, I gave a reception at Sherry's, and invited a large company to meet some distinguished artist friends who had promised me to sing. These comprised Madame Gadski, Madame Schumann-Heink, M. Alvarez, and Mr. van Rooy, with Miss Esther Palliser and Mr. David Bispham to represent American art. When it was too late, I discovered to my surprise (not unmingled with amusement) that I had attempted a Quixotic feat. The talent was too strong for the occasion.

Almost any one of these artists, appearing unaided and alone at a recital, would have filled Carnegie Hall. But as a group they were too overwhelming. They were individually all ready and anxious to sing for me, as an old friend, and most of them did so. Not the two prima donnas, however ;

they were afraid of extinguishing each other's light.   As for the guests, I heard afterwards that they had openly expressed amazement at the wanton waste and extravagance of crowding so many celebrities into one programme.

When I gave my next reception a year later I took care not to mix my stars.   On that occasion only one shone forth, but he a very brilliant one, in the person of my old friend Ignaz Paderewski, then in New York for the production of his opera " Manru." He was generosity itself.   He sat down to the piano and stayed there, playing piece after piece, for nearly an hour and a half.   Moreover, when his compatriot, Timothée Adamowski, took up his violin to perform a selection from the new opera, Paderewski insisted upon playing his accompaniment, although they had never re-hearsed together.   That day my amateur guests made an enthusiastic crowd, and the subsequent comments, so far as I could learn, were entirely of a laudatory nature.

Personal experiences generally afford the

most reliable evidence, and of these I encountered an abundance whilst endeavouring
to gauge the depth of amateur musical intelli-
gence in New York. It varied considerably,
of course ; but, speaking frankly, I am bound
to say I found the average shallower than one
would have anticipated in a city where there
is such a wealth of splendid music, for the
most part splendidly given.

The reasons for this will appear later. For
the moment let it suffice to say that the individual amateur is much less concerned with
works than with performers, with operas than
with singers, with orchestras than with conductors. From first to last it is the " personal
equation " that carries most weight ; and even
that may lose some of its potency if the
amateur line of vision, requiring as it does
an extremely easy and limited focus, be dis-
turbed by the introduction of more than one
central figure. A central group, as we have
already seen, is practically out of the question.

The curious mental attitude of the New York
amateur in this regard was again demonstrated

when I gave a series of Sunday Popular Concerts at the new German Theatre during the winter of 1908–9. My idea was to bring good artists together for the performance of chamber music, to introduce talent, both known and unknown, of a high order, to give the American composer a chance of being heard, and to encourage the singing of songs in the language of the people.

Against the artistic success of my experiment not a word was ever urged. I was only told, in print and otherwise, that "if I persevered for three or four years at a possible loss of twelve or fifteen thousand dollars, I might ultimately convert my 'excellent' concerts into a financial success." I gave nineteen in all, on consecutive Sunday afternoons, and then held out no longer. The amateurs had been thirsty for a star. If I insisted on putting two or three stars into the same bill every week, then through the very act of conjoining them I made them stars no longer.*

* This reference to my Sunday Concerts would not be complete without an expression of gratitude to those genuine lovers

This inordinate and insatiable demand for a star is the curse of the dramatic and musical stage in America. It engenders that incessant yearning for the sensational to which impresarios, managers, and concert-givers, with their

of good music and kind friends who so generously gave me substantial help when the enterprise most needed it. Many distinguished people, it is true, were content to give their names as patrons and no more. But there were several subscribers for boxes and stalls—among them Mrs. George Gould, Mrs. Paul Morton, Mr. and Mrs. Otto H. Kahn, Mr. and Mrs. S. R. Guggenheim, Mr. Melville Stone, Mr. and Mrs. Walter Luttgen, Mr. and Mrs. Fritz Achelis, Mr. and Mrs. George Place, Mr. and Mrs. I. N. Spiegelberg, Mr. J. M. Lichtenauer, Mr. and Mrs. Siegfried Prince, and Mr. and Mrs. Peter Zucker.

Then, later on, when I had lost a large sum by the concerts, I was advised by my friends to form a guarantee fund to help to meet any further deficit in connection with the first season's efforts. To this request for aid a noble response was made by, among others, Mr. Andrew Carnegie, Mrs. Clarence Mackay, the late Mrs. Jesse Seligman, Mr. S. R. Guggenheim, Mr. Francis S. Loring, Mr. Otto Kahn, Mr. J. W. Spalding, Mr. E. J. de Coppet, Mr. Ernst Thalmann, Mr. I. N. Spiegelberg, Mr. William Salomon, Mr. Arthur Leland, Mr. J. D. Higgins, and Mr. W. H. Taylor. Still my personal loss on the season of nineteen concerts amounted, notwithstanding this aid, to several thousand dollars.

I shall have something to say further in this book upon the question of New York Concert Guarantee Funds. So far as my own experience goes they are supported by true amateurs of good music, whose sole inducement is to encourage the growth and development of the Art in its highest manifestations.

natural eye for the dollars and cents, feel themselves compelled to pander.   In New York especially, the very hot-bed of the star-system, they must either cater to and for it— or starve.

IV.—CONCERNING NEW YORK AUDIENCES

A NEW York audience loves to look upon itself as the most critical in the world. It is taught to believe that it is ; but I venture to assert that it is nothing of the sort. It knows whether it is pleased or not ; but that is a very different thing from knowing upon what standards of artistic judgment its criticism is based ; very different from manifesting that knowledge with conviction and authority.

Nay, seeking primarily to be entertained, it yields too readily to the emotion of the moment, and allows itself to be diverted by the superficial qualities of what it is listening to. In a word, it is impressionable and receptive, not analytical or severe. In reality, therefore, it is an indulgent public.

This is to some extent reflected in its attitude towards artists, whether in the opera-house or the concert-room. It is invariably courteous, sympathetic, cordial, and kind. Never once so long as I was in New York did I hear an audience hiss or " boo " at a performer, or indulge in any direct manifestation of impatience or displeasure. Silence or an early departure may occasionally have been intended to fulfil the latter purpose ; but many a time did I look for these polite indications of feeling when they were eminently deserved—in vain. On the other hand, when it is pleased or amused no audience could be more swift to bestow its guerdon of spontaneous and enthusiastic applause.

Politeness and indulgence in the attitude of an audience are not unwelcome characteristics. Neither do they necessarily betray ignorance as to the real merits of a composition or an artist. But the trained musician who instantly recognizes the true value of what he is hearing can never be mistaken about the critical capacity of the assemblage whereof he forms a unit. He divines it as by instinct. He feels it in the atmosphere. He can tell whether the applause rings true or not—whether there was a shade more or less than the occasion warranted.

The attitude or opinion of the individual is another matter. Converse for five minutes with a typical New York music-lover—especially one of the fair sex—and, if words can convey it, you will receive an impression of lofty ideals, of exalted standards, of what the Germans call *Schwärmerei* anent art and artists, that will cause your soul to rejoice. A closer acquaintance will very possibly modify your sensations of joy.

I met with many such examples. Here and there, it is true, I came across an enthusiast who revealed the unmistakable attributes of the veritable connoisseur. But for one such I came across at least a dozen in whom this display of verbal eclecticism and gushing superficialities amounted to nothing more than a "pose." The stream quickly runs dry. Your interlocutor speedily deserts the subject in hand for an effusive outpouring concerning something or somebody else.

Criticism of a singer or an executant is almost always in the nature of a comparison. For example : you ask a young lady what she thinks of Pachmann ; she answers, " Pachmann plays Chopin very well, but I prefer Paderewski, —he is so much greater all round ! "

Again : " Do I like Tetrazzini ? Oh, immensely ; but she only makes her ' hit ' in old Italian operas and phonograph records. Guess she daren't come down off the stage and sing a whole recital at Carnegie, like Sembrich. Oh, Sembrich's *great!* "

Or again : " Yes, Mahler is a fine conductor —just as intellectual as he can be. But, say, imagine what he *would* be if for once he could *feel* an opera like Campanini ! Now, if he'd only throw down his bâton and shake his fist at his orchestra like Safonoff, why he'd drive me crazy ! " Always the same subtle anxiety to show that people and things can be a little better than they are.

The newest word in modern music is not

too new for the New Yorker, be its meaning ever so obscure. Like the latest fashion in hats, its vast proportions and downright ugliness (when it is ugly) are forgotten in the delirious joy of its eccentricity and the possible charm of what is concealed beneath its spreading surface. Is it really understood, really enjoyed ?

The kind of person already quoted has the same superlatives for Richard Strauss as for Richard Wagner, for Camille Saint-Saëns as for Max Reger, for Mahler as for Debussy. Apparently the English language does not supply nuances enough for purposes of differentiation.

Strauss, Saint-Saëns, and Mahler all paid their first visits to America during the period of my residence there. Never, perhaps, did three musicians of the same epoch write or comport themselves in more contrasted fashions. The New York amateur " tarred them all with the same brush." The real modesty of Saint-Saëns, the false modesty of Mahler, and the immodesty of Strauss evoked identical outbursts of admiration.

American audiences as a whole are wonderfully quick to feel and respond to the mood of an artist. They are lively, alert, appreciative : filled with magnetism themselves, and ready to recognize temperament and magnetism in the performer. A more delightful public to sing or play before I have never encountered.

It is a pity they are so inclined to be unpunctual. An opera or a concert in New York rarely begins till ten minutes or a quarter of an hour after the advertised time. At the opera late-comers are trooping in all through the first act. At a concert they apparently time their arrival so as to be kept waiting at the doors ; for nearly half the occupants of the stalls or parquet do not come in until the overture or the first movement of the symphony or quartet has been played.

In compensation, be it said, they are fast cultivating the habit of remaining in their places until the last chord has sounded, instead of disturbing the music by rushing off to secure carriages and catch trains after the unseemly English custom.

The audiences at the Metropolitan Opera House comprise a far more extensive proportion of New York aristocracy than those frequenting the Manhattan. They are not more discriminating because of that ; but they are less prone to give their feelings outward expression. Just as at Covent Garden, the real amateurs of opera are to be found in the cheaper parts of the house ; and from them comes the cue for those genuine outbursts of applause which the *habitué* can never confound with the noisy, impertinent interruptions of the *claque*.

If the bejewelled patronesses of the parterre boxes really loved opera, they and their friends would assuredly leave the dinner-table a little earlier. As it is they arrive late, especially on a Wagner night. They evince an apparently slight interest in the stage. They contribute but a meagre share towards the applause, unless a Sembrich or a Caruso be singing, when they can grow as frantic with excitement and split gloves as recklessly as the most impetuous of their sex.

At the Manhattan—a much smaller house—

the average temperament of the audiences is less frigid, and enthusiasm is more easily aroused. There, however, traditions date back no farther than three or four seasons. When people of wealth and social position began going to the new house in Thirty-fourth Street, it was obviously not for the purpose of staring at each other, but ot enjoying the opera. They have continued to adhere to that intent, even if they have since then become subscribers or regular attendants.

Go to which house you will, though, the Metropolitan or the Manhattan, it is not the genius of the composer (excepting always Wagner) nor the unadorned beauty of his creation, nor the priceless perfection of the ensemble, that you are assisting to celebrate with the incense of your applause and the sweet spice of your dollars.

It is the eternal and everlasting glorification of the Star.

V.—HOW NATIVE TALENT IS TREATED

A SHORT time before my departure from New York I met a well-known American musician, whose name was frequently being mentioned just then as a coming operatic composer. He stopped to shake hands and wish me *bon voyage*.

"I hear you are leaving this city," he said, expressing regret. "But for one reason I am glad. After your long stay you will be able to write a book about music here, and, among other things, let the world know how shamefully American musicians are neglected and ignored in their own land."

"Do you imagine," I asked, "that America is the only country which is guilty of that particular crime?"

"Assuredly not," replied my friend. "Only here in New York it seems to me that we are treated rather worse than the English musician, for instance, is treated in London ; certainly a hundred times worse than the native musician in Paris or Berlin or Vienna. Over there one gets a chance, but on this side, where the patriotic note is ever sounding, the last person to obtain an entrance, much less a footing, at the opera or in the concert-room is the American composer."

"How about American artists ? "

"Ah, you are perhaps even more familiar with that end of the story than I am. I only know that it is as a composer I have most reason to complain. If I send in a score of an opera to the Metropolitan or the Manhattan, it is returned in due course with a letter of regret. If I ask for an 'audition' I am informed that the director has no time to spare for the purpose, or that there is no demand for opera in English. If I declare that I am willing to have my opera sung in any language under the sun, I am politely shut up with the information that the patrons of grand opera in New York are not looking, anyhow, for works by untried American composers."

" That may mean that if you could succeed in winning European fame first, you might stand a chance of a production here ? "

" Most likely ; but not even then, I fancy, unless I could bring strong social influence to bear. I do hear that one or two popular Americans are being asked to write operas for the Manhattan, but they are men with ' pull ' on their side and who have probably been waiting twenty years for their chance."

" What do you intend to do ? "

" Oh, try Europe, I suppose. There, at any rate, my nationality will not stand in the way, and I shall get a little encouragement if I deserve it."

And with that we parted.

The question of the treatment of native musicians is one which does not reflect discreditably upon New York alone, but upon the whole of the United States.

Years ago it became an established convention, nay, an unwritten law, that every American who aspired to high rank as a singer or instrumentalist must go through the final course of study in Europe, and there obtain the *cachet* of approval and success before submitting his or her claims to the consideration of an American audience.

This custom dies hard ; and very natural it is that it should. American students only have confidence in their home teachers down to a certain point, beyond which they feel the need for the supreme touch of a famous master or mistress of the day, and for the " atmosphere " of European musical life. American audiences, it would seem, have no confidence in their own judgment, unless it has first been indicated for them by opinions carried home from abroad and intensified by all the flowery superlatives that a resourceful press agent can supply.

The attitude of the press in this matter I shall come to later on. Let us merely note that in the case of the native *début*, as in every other, it is the verdict of New York that " cuts the ice." Europe—New York—the tour East and West—such is the route that the American aspirant to musical fame must inevitably traverse.

A peculiar feature of the toilsome journey is the fact that, whilst recognition of exceptional ability in home-bred artists is slowly and grudgingly vouchsafed, nothing can exceed the patriotic pride of their fellow-countrymen directly they have arrived anywhere near the top rung of the ladder. It may be said without fear of contradiction that every swan now floating proudly upon the waters of American popularity has at some time in the past been a neglected "ugly duckling," despised and rejected of critics and acquainted with discouragement.

It is easy to be wise after the event; it is even pleasant to reward successful artists with appreciation, if with nothing more substantial, after all the difficulties have been surmounted. Do wealthy Americans, I wonder, ever dream of what they might do to foster and educate the musical talent that abounds in almost every section of their great country ? They boast loudly enough of their love for good music. A few of them bestow generous support upon individual native musicians. A still smaller number contribute modest sums (or lend money without security, to be repaid when convenient) towards the cost of training promising students.

But compare these tiny benefactions with the colossal amounts annually given and bequeathed by the millionaires to swell university funds, to endow professional " chairs," to build and fill libraries ; in fact, to aid the cause of education in every way except by providing means to develop the gifts of the impecunious musical genius. Really, as it seems to me, the idea that such a thing is possible, that it can accomplish a vast deal of good, that the helping of youthful artists on their upward road is a far more beneficial act than the bestowal of indiscriminate charity, never occurs to the Crœsuses of the Western hemisphere.

Yet, I ought not to say " never ; " for during my stay in New York there came to my knowledge several instances of generosity on the part of individual lovers of the art—patrons and supporters in the true sense of the word. These are worthy replicas of distinguished European families like the Rothschilds, the Montefiores, and the Goldsmids, who have for a century or more taken delight in defraying the cost of educating musically their talented but needy co-religionists.

Rather ought I to express regret that this splendid example is not more widely imitated, alike in New York and the other big cities where they scamper around to find sites to build opera-houses and look across the ocean for singers to fill them.

But does it follow, because these places lavish millions on their opera-houses and their orchestras, that they are actually doing the best that can be done for music as a phase of national art?

New York, for example, spends the most extravagant sums on its " stars." It has taken to subscribing thousands of dollars to capitalize its orchestras.   It maintains its musical luxuries upon a scale calculated to make Uncle Sam's bosom positively burst with pride.

But it will not dip its hand one inch deeper into its pockets than London or Paris to go to concerts or to listen to " unstarred " artists, whether new or old, American or European. As to supporting music purely for the Art's sake, it will do absolutely nothing unless through personal canvass and individual persuasion.   To begin to compare it in this respect with smaller European cities such as Manchester, Hamburg, Frankfort, Munich, Leipsic, and Brussels, where the demand for good music is the equivalent of a daily necessity—that would be supremely absurd !

To speak of New York, therefore, as an essentially musical city is to proclaim it that which it is not.   It is a place where there is much music, and where more money is now spent on music than anywhere else in the world.

The musical season begins in October and continues without interruption until the end of

April. Opera is going on from the middle of November until the end of March. Counting Brooklyn as part of New York, there may be as many as eighteen operatic representations and thirty concerts taking place per week during the greater part of this period—an approximate total of, say, 350 performances of opera and 650 concerts during the entire season. For a city of five million inhabitants (counting in Greater New York) this would not be excessive if, let me say, one-tenth of the population were sufficiently musical to care to pay to listen to good music. One-tenth would be 500,000. As a matter of fact, not one-tenth of *that* tenth (or one in every hundred of the population) can be counted among the people who periodically pay from ten cents to two dollars to go to a concert in New York.

There are said to be 20,000 professional musicians in the city, more than half of whom are teachers. No one supposes that professional musicians pay to go to a concert ! Very few of them care, even if they can afford it, to pay to hear an opera.

Amidst this hurly-burly of clashing entertainments what chance can there possibly be
for the unknown or unheralded new-comer?
Here the dividing-line between the native and
the foreign artist should be sharply drawn.   It
is right to protest if New York discourages and
neglects the American musician ; but it would
be unjust to complain because this vast Empire
City pays scant attention to the procession of
débutants that cross the Atlantic every year to
seek fame and fortune in the United States.

What else can be expected?

Average New Yorkers take no interest
whatever in names with which they are not
familiar.   They have quite enough to do to
hear artists whom they already know and
admire.   The press-agent and the manager
may work like Trojans (and they certainly will
do so if it be made worth their while) ; but to
arouse more than a very limited amount of
interest and curiosity concerning a stranger is
what they term a " tough proposition."

Consequently, much depends upon the circumstances — I should   perhaps   add,   the

" auspices "—of the *début*. The standing or reputation of the new-comer, the nature of the preliminary boom, and last, but not least, the proportion of friends and " deadheads " among the audience, may possibly affect the ultimate verdict almost as materially as the talent of the artist.

But to return to the question of the native musician. He has a hard battle to fight, whatever his country, and it ought not to be made harder for him in America than elsewhere. On the contrary, it should actually be easier to get on—provided there be real talent *au fond*—in this land of magnificent distances, untold riches, and immeasurable resources.

In Europe we may be justified in speaking of the musical profession as overcrowded. In America it is not so, and will not be for many a day to come. There is, at least, plenty of room still for the home product if it be of the right quality. It should not merely be cultivated ; it should be encouraged and stimulated by methods not less direct than those employed for the protection of native industries.

I have never advocated placing the claims of nationality before those of Art, and in the choice of a musician I should be guided solely by the thought of securing the best. But, given two musicians of equal merit, I should not hesitate to choose the one native to the soil. America is so generous in offering a home to the " foreigner " that she could well afford to establish, if not a " tariff reform," at least some kind of preference in the employment of her own composers and artists. The Musical Union can be depended upon to look after the orchestral players.

New York, of course, is overcrowded with musicians. So, I dare say, are some of the other big cities. The United States, as a whole, is not ; and one has only to glance at the wonderful work—wonderful both as to quantity and quality—now going on in musical circles in the South and to the West of the Mississippi, to realize that in this, as so many other departments of life and art, the country is still in its infancy.

VI.—INSTITUTIONS AND THEIR EXPLOITERS

I HAVE thus far described conditions as they appear upon the surface of musical life in New York. If we would examine causes we must probe deeper, and study the underlying factors in a situation which is as full of contradictions as the evidence in an Irish action for damages.

To ascertain what the tree is really like we must either cut clean through it or strip off the bark completely. Then only can we perceive how much of it is good honest wood, how much a mixture of gnarled knots and—rotten core!

America is justly proud of her institutions, more particularly of those which serve for the education and instruction of the people. Strange it is that a country which has developed

45

so magnificently in some respects should have lingered so far behind in others. "Give us time!" is the cry I have always heard, whenever I have pointed out the unfairness of the proportion between the liberal provision for the advancement of Science and the absolute *nil* that contemptuously dismisses the Arts of Music and the Drama.

"Give us time; we are a young country!" Yes, that is very well. But since the days of George Washington much water has flowed beneath the bridges, and "God's country" has gone ahead so rapidly in certain things that it has no right to shirk responsibilities or make excuses regarding those which appeal less vividly to the national imagination and the public sense of duty.

Music receives no support whatever from the State in America, and there seems to be little likelihood of its doing so for many a day to come. I suppose the senator of the present era who should have the effrontery to rise in his place—not at Washington, perhaps, but at Albany or Boston (this would hardly be a

Federal matter, anyhow)—and propose that the State of New York or Massachusetts devote half a million dollars yearly to the cause of musical education—that worthy legislator would assuredly be suspected of insanity, if not something worse.

I once asked a prominent politician to give me his views on this subject. He replied, " I only know that opera and the theatres seem to prosper abundantly without extraneous aid of any kind, and who knows but that the State stepping in might do more harm than good! I am told that New York has too much music as it is, and, in my opinion, neither the city nor the State has need to concern itself with the business of higher musical education."

Doubtless, this was a fair sample of the general idea. Nor did I once during my stay in America come across a "representative of the people" who displayed any real familiarity with the question or appeared to regard it as coming within the region of practical legislation —and politics.

With the political or national institutions of America I am not, however, concerned. What I now have to say refers to those exclusively musical institutions, semi-public, semi-private, which carry on the executive work of this great Art in the largest city of the United States.

And they all of them have this in common : that, no matter how admirable they may be in fundamental principle, no matter how excellently devised for the general good of humanity, their noblest purposes may be thwarted, their machinery upset and dislocated, their credit besmirched and brought into disrepute, through the shortcomings and selfishness of those whose privilege it is to superintend or carry on their functions.

In New York I had exceptional chances for studying both musical institutions and musical men ; and I was compelled by degrees to form the solid conviction that, in nine cases out of ten where there was cause for dissatisfaction, it was the men and not the institutions that were to blame.

To blame—in what way ? For failing, not

through ignorance or carelessness, but, I repeat, through simple selfishness, to place before all else their consideration for the dignity, the honour, the true welfare, the permanent good, of the particular institution with which they were associated.

I believe that the form of selfishness to which I refer in this instance is more than anything else the outcome of vanity.

Selfishness and vanity are the most striking and prominent ingredients of the New York character. The lust for power, the struggle for reputation, the craving for notoriety, the restless desire to be always just ahead of the next man—these defects of the otherwise splendid American nature assert themselves, unfortunately, among the leaders and counsellors of musical life in New York even more strongly than among the rank and file of the profession.

Happily there are exceptions—men and women who work for sheer love of good music or the particular branch of it in which they are most keenly interested. I could name a few whose untiring devotion and singleness of

E

purpose have, to my knowledge, contrasted strongly with the selfish aims of their associates on the same boards of direction. In these cases intrigue and strategy carry the day. The "wheels within wheels" are ably concealed, and what appears to be a disinterested proposition is often a deeply-laid scheme of action skilfully carried through.

To attempt to define more minutely the curious motives that lie behind these intrigues would be a waste of time. With some it is thirst for position and power ; with others a desire for a more sordid reward ; but with all, or nearly all, the yearning to satisfy the cravings of that vanity which Jane Austen has made one of the characters in "Pride and Prejudice," describe as relating "to what we would have others think of us."

Roughly speaking, musical existence and enterprise in New York may be separated into four main channels. Their courses are quite distinct. They can scarcely be said to approach each other at any given point ; never by any chance closely enough for their currents to be united and furnish mutual support.

Each of these " channels " is well stocked with fish of every size and variety, ranging from the minnows of the profession up to the salmon and the tarpon. The former are not always immune from the attacks of the genus labelled " ferox " ; but that is inevitable, being indeed a common experience all over the world. It does occasionally happen, however, that a remarkably fine fish, endowed with trout-like leaping powers, contrives to jump from one " channel " into another. The feat, when it is accomplished, is generally due to the strange propinquity of Church and Stage.

The main channels referred to comprise (1) Opera, (2) Concerts, (3) Church Choirs, and (4) Musical Culture.

Each of these should have its progress regulated, its interests guarded, by representative institutions. The first and second are thus aided and protected. The third and fourth are not.

Then, in addition to the channels, there is

a kind of intersecting canal, not directly connected with any of them, yet in a measure influencing their courses. This canal, which derives its own current (or, rather, receives tributary streams) from each of the channels, and in return helps to guide, push, retard, or scold them on their way—is a figurative embodiment of the function performed by the newspaper press of New York City.

Behind the institutions stand the men who exploit them. Behind the newspapers stand their musical critics. How do they actually fulfil their various tasks ?

I shall have herein to deal less with general conditions and rather more with individuals. I will therefore ask the reader to accompany me " behind the scenes," whilst I try to give him a glimpse of some of the personages who were or are responsible for the present situation in this interesting musical evolution.

Let us begin with Opera.

VII.—AUTOCRATS OF THE OPERA HOUSE

MAURICE GRAU

THERE is nothing essentially national, or even peculiarly American, about the operatic "craze" which has been raging in New York for the past four or five years and is now extending to other Eastern cities. It confers no particular blessing upon the country. It does much for foreign and very little for native singers.

It contributes but slightly towards the inculcation and crystallization of those exalted ideals which are essential to the real growth and development of this universal Art. It just shows that the people are at heart fond of music and especially partial to the lyric stage. The Opera will surely endure ; but how long the "craze" will last remains to be seen !

53

During my eight seasons in New York the Metropolitan Opera House was governed by four impresarios. Of these, two are dead; and the other two are still endeavouring, at the time this is written, to decide which of them is the real head of the establishment.

The first of the quartet, Maurice Grau, I knew very intimately. He was associated with the late Sir Augustus Harris in the direction of Covent Garden. He afterwards became its managing director, and only resigned that post when the work of carrying on two of the largest opera houses in the world became too heavy for him.

Under Grau, Opera in New York did what it had done under Harris in London. It assumed an international character. It replaced a "hand to mouth" policy by a systematic organization; above all, it attracted the support of society and became the recognized resort of fashion.

For a time the same artists used to appear at both opera houses. The history of a Covent Garden season in the summer was the history of the Metropolitan Opera House in the following winter and spring. I am aware that New Yorkers then imagined it was the other way about; they were told, and they began to believe, that London was following in their footsteps. But, whatever may have happened since, that was not the case in Grau's day.

Maurice Grau was not an originator; he was an excellent imitator. He combined just enough of the artistic with his commercial instincts and training to earn the confidence of the wealthy business magnates who supported his enterprise. He contrived, moreover, to make opera pay without losing the manners of a gentleman.

I remember seeing him at Windsor Castle on the occasion of the last "command" performance of opera that Queen Victoria was destined to witness—it was only a few months before her death. As I glanced at him when standing beside Earl de Grey in the St. George's Hall, wearing his knee-breeches and black silk stockings, I said to myself, How strange!

That keen American manager does not look a bit out of place here in his Windsor uniform, waiting to receive the Queen of England !

The disposition and behaviour of the man were reflected in the internal *régime* of his opera house. His artists respected and loved him. They were aware that he could drive a close bargain ; but they also knew they could rely upon his word—and so did the public. There was no friction. The wheels went round smoothly. The various nationalities got on pretty well together.

If there was ever trouble among the prima donnas, I am bound to say it was chiefly confined to the Americans, who were then climbing to the top of the tree. Jealous to a degree, and gifted with the very genius of intrigue, it was wonderful how resolutely those ladies fought for the limelight and the centre of the stage. And either they or their successors are doing the same thing still !

Nevertheless, in Grau's time one might observe a healthy tone, a spirit of "live and let live," a certain evidence of artistic forethought and consideration that have disappeared from New York opera of to-day.

Solid strength and all-round brilliancy have notably diminished with the gradual admixture of talent of another order. The *mise en scène* has improved; orchestral effects are more carefully studied; the choruses are larger and better trained. But the casts, the ensembles, save in the case of a few specially prepared works, cannot claim the artistic importance, the rare constellations of vocal genius, or the perfection of finish (whatever they may represent in dollars) that they boasted in the days of Maurice Grau and the De Reszkes.

I hear the cry of "*laudator temporis acti!*" It does not in the least disturb me. People with short memories and members of a younger generation are wont to raise it directly such comparisons are made. But to a veteran whose recollections of opera go back to the "halcyon days" of Patti, Nilsson, Tietjens, Lucca, Trebelli, Scalchi, Campanini, Gayarre, Masini, Tamagno, Faure, Graziani, Foli, and other giants of the "seventies," these New

York experiences are but as the events of yesterday.

I spent a memorable fortnight in New York in the spring of 1896, and was present at the Metropolitan on the interesting night when " Lohengrin " was given with Nordica, Marie Brema, Jean de Reszke and Edouard de Reszke ; on which occasion, by the way, Madame Nordica's friends presented her, on the conclusion of the performance, with a diamond tiara.   That was at the climax of Abbey-Grau administration, and neither for brilliancy nor beauty of execution has the representation been surpassed during the last decade.

Operatic salaries have gone up since then.* The leading " stars " are more costly ; but I venture with all respect to question whether they are even worth half as much as their immediate predecessors.   Apart from Luisa

* They are said to have nearly doubled, whilst the prices of admission remain practically the same.   The keen competition between the two New York opera houses for the services of the principal singers has sent the salary list up to fabulous heights, with an effect upon the treasury that is simply disastrous.

Tetrazzini, Emma Destinn, and Enrico Caruso, who stand in a class by themselves, the popular operatic idols of to-day are not, in the true sense of the term, great opera singers. And in saying this I naturally exclude from the comparison prima donnas such as Melba, Sembrich, Nordica, and Eames, who, although they are still singing, would scarcely proclaim their voices to be what they were during the Grau period of management.

Anyhow, figures are misleading. It is absurd to argue, because opera companies are larger, because they cost double what they did, and draw from the public larger aggregate sums in a season, that the splendour and efficiency of the establishment have had no parallel in the past.

I assert, on the contrary, that notwithstanding certain mechanical improvements in the stage and minor details and other points above noted, the performances at the Metropolitan no longer reveal the standard of supreme excellence that they boasted in the lifetime of Maurice Grau.

Heinrich Conried

The deterioration began with the advent in 1903 of the late Heinrich Conried, an Austrian actor who had shown ability in the management of the New York German Theatre. Mr. Conried, supported by the German banking element of the city, made his way to the directorship of the Metropolitan knowing no more about opera than an ordinary chauffeur knows about aeroplanes.

But his ignorance did not outstrip either his indomitable energy or his colossal self-reliance. I am not sure which of these qualities it was that most justified his friends' belief in him. I recollect, however, an observation made by one of these friends which struck me very much at the time, to the effect that if Conried " could only rid himself of the petty ideas of economy which he had cultivated at the German Theatre, he might do very well at the Metropolitan."

He did do well—for himself.   He went to

his new post a man of comparatively limited means. For his first season he tried, as his friends had feared, to work the economical policy. But this was more than the millionaire stockholders and directors, or even the German bankers, would permit him to try for long.

He certainly endeavoured to win Jean de Reszke back to America for his opening season. That I know for a fact, because one day I met Mr. Conried when crossing from Dover to Calais, and, as we went on to Paris together, he, not being acquainted with the famous tenor, entrusted to me the delicate mission of negotiating terms with him for forty appearances in America. I went to see M. de Reszke (in June, 1903), but he positively refused to go back to New York or, indeed, to sing for Mr. Conried at any price.

The investment which the new impresario was not allowed the chance of making in this direction was diverted to that of "Parsifal." Here he "struck oil." Heinrich Conried was not naturally a polite man. Indeed, it was his habit, when opposed by a stronger or crushing a weaker will than his own, to adopt a manner that was extremely objectionable. It was not surprising, therefore, when Frau Cosima Wagner refused him permission to produce " Parsifal " in America, that he made a few offensive remarks about that lady and proceeded to appropriate the treasure of Bayreuth without her leave.

Of course it was a huge success. Why not ? The utter and complete novelty of the thing ; the delightful sense of piratical freedom from mere copyright law ; the overwhelming beauty of the work, and the really creditable manner of its presentation—all tended to ensure one of those tremendous sensations which in America spell fortune. Giving " Parsifal " in New York " without leave " was an inspiration ; and Heinrich Conried made a hundred thousand dollars by it.

Moreover, it rendered his appointment secure and it emboldened him to play for higher stakes. It encouraged him to engage for the following season some of the prima donnas whom he had economically omitted from his preliminary list. It enabled him to conclude an engagement with Signor Caruso (whose contract for the Metropolitan he had inherited from Maurice Grau) to sing for him exclusively for a term of years at a price never previously paid to a tenor.

It inspired him, too, with another idea—the production for the first time in New York of Strauss's "Salome." * For Mr. Conried, having begun by inoculating his operatic public with a taste for the sensational, found himself obliged, not altogether against his will, to feed them upon " sensations " and little else.

Certain high-sounding promises about founding an " American School of Operatic Art " at the Metropolitan Opera House, with which Mr. Conried had started out, were only partially fulfilled. The school was established, but badly managed ; it was expected to pay its own way, which of course was out of the

---

* "Salome" was performed just once, on the occasion of Mr. Conried's annual benefit, on January 22, 1907. Its repetition was forbidden.

question. It merely served as a feeder for
the chorus and to supply flower maidens for
" Parsifal " at nominal salaries. It attracted a
few good voices, but accomplished nothing of
permanent value, and generally left "American
operatic art " where it had previously been.

Indeed, on behalf of native singers, in my
estimation, Mr. Henry W. Savage achieved
results infinitely more valuable by his English
production of " Parsifal " than Mr. Conried
did during his whole period of government
at the Metropolitan. One can scarcely name
an American member of the " triple cast " that
took part in Mr. Savage's " Parsifal " who is
not to-day a prominent artist at a leading
opera house in Germany, Austria, and the
United States. One or two of them have
sung with success at Covent Garden, and, if
the principal Parsifal was a German, at least
the principal Kundry was an Englishwoman —
to wit, Mme. Kirkby Lunn.

To return to Mr. Conried. That lucky yet
unlucky manager's star was not to remain long
in the ascendant. Three big troubles in quick

succession are supposed to have contributed to the mental worries which culminated in an attack of paralysis, and, after the season of 1907–8, brought the Conried reign to a conclusion.

One of these troubles was the heavy pecuniary loss sustained through the destruction of scenery and property in the San Francisco earthquake ; another was caused by the annoying arrest of Signor Caruso ; and the third was the refusal of the New York police authorities to allow " Salome " to be repeated after the first performance.

In the spring of 1909 Heinrich Conried died.

OSCAR HAMMERSTEIN

Now, had Mr. Conried never lived to be director of the Metropolitan Opera House, I do not think we should have ever seen aught of the so-called " Opera war " which started in New York at about the midway of his *régime* (that is to say, in the autumn of 1906), and is now in active progress.

F

I do not think we should have ever beheld another manager so "exceeding bold" as to start a second opera house at full grand opera prices, without the pledged support of society, without the Metropolitan "Horseshoe" of tiaras and diamonds representing millions of dollars ; and, above all, at a new theatre situated in an inferior part of the town.

But there was a man in New York with aspirations in this direction, and he, undaunted by his own record of previous operatic failures, seems to have thus reasoned with himself—

"This is my opportunity. Surely I know more about opera than Conried does. At any rate, I can profit by his mistakes. He has been doing no good with Italian Opera. I will make it my speciality. I will engage great artists whom he has left out in the cold. I will make Conried a present of Caruso and German Opera, and after that what is there that New Yorkers care about ?—'Faust,' 'Carmen,' and Puccini—that's all. American Opera by native composers ? Not for them or me ! No, I'll try Italian Opera on the grand scale.

That's what they want; and if the Four
Hundred would like it, they can come to
Thirty-fourth Street, and enjoy it too ! "

Coming from the manager of a variety
theatre, celebrated as a builder of new theatres,
as the amateur composer of a comic opera, and
as the inventor of clever contrivances for cigar-
making, the announcement of the opening of
the Manhattan Opera House by Mr. Oscar
Hammerstein was received by the public with
interest and by society with incredulity and
derision. Curiosity was chiefly concentrated
upon the question : Whose money is at the
back of the venture ? People refused to
believe it was Mr. Hammerstein's ; but to this
day they have never discovered that it was put
up by any one else.

The new scheme was, nevertheless, destined
to exercise an important and far-reaching
influence upon operatic methods in New York.
It was to awaken the somnolent directors of
the Metropolitan to the fact that there was
room in that swelling metropolis for more than
one opera house. It was to teach them that,

whatever their hold upon society, they commanded neither a monopoly of great artists nor an exclusive control of the suffrages of the opera-loving public.

For a long time they refused to take it seriously. All through the first season they gave no sign of regarding it as an opposition worth reckoning with. They did not know their man.

They did not realize that Oscar Hammerstein actually knew more about opera than Heinrich Conried ; that he could play the impresario to good purpose by sitting in the wings at every performance, watching rehearsals without interfering with them, talking genially to his visitors (so long as he thought them useful), and, above all, keeping a " weather-eye " open for the best European talent that his opponents had overlooked.

One day, at a *matinée* performance, I was conversing with Mr. Hammerstein on the stage when I saw approaching my old friend Mr. Otto Kahn, the chairman of the Executive Board of the Metropolitan Opera House—an ardent and genuine lover of the art—whose parents I had known intimately before I went to live in New York.

To see Mr. Kahn at the Manhattan was something of a surprise. So, too, was his request: " Will you be good enough to introduce me to Mr. Hammerstein ? " I complied with unfeigned pleasure, and left them to make each other's better acquaintance.*

Then I knew the awakening had come ; that the Metropolitan directors had taken a proper measurement of the man who had metaphorically snapped his fingers at them.

Mr. Hammerstein was fortunate to be in a position to utilize the names of Mme. Melba and Edouard de Reszke as a lever for the raising up of a new and first-class opera company (though poor Edouard, alas ! never got to the Manhattan) ; fortunate also to obtain the countenance and support of Mrs. Clarence

* The acquaintanceship did not, I believe, ripen into friendship. How could it ? After a brief interchange of courtesies, the two managements resumed their pleasant task of competing for each other's artists and have continued at war ever since.

Mackay, a lady of considerable artistic taste and intuition, who, mortally tired of the methods in vogue at the Metropolitan, was only too glad to see some one strong and defiant enough to set up in opposition on lines of possible reform.

Still, the well-nigh unanimous opinion was that the new enterprise would result in a disastrous failure. I was with the minority who thought otherwise. At about this time Mr. Hammerstein favoured me with a good deal of his confidence. I saw that he was in deadly earnest. He was a born purveyor of sensations, and he had carefully studied the weak points in his fellow-citizens. His expenses were enormous. Society, barring Mrs. Mackay, refused to cross from Fifth to Eighth Avenue. The Italians proved half-hearted till Mme. Melba arrived ; then she, and after her Madame Calvé, saved the situation.

Instead of going bankrupt, the new impresario lost only a few thousand dollars on the season. He also found a veritable " star " conductor in Cleofonte Campanini, who for three years tyrannized delightfully over the entire establishment, insisting on conducting every opera, refusing to brook a rival, influencing the choice of most of the artists ; in short, inserting a huge finger in every pie.

Naturally, New York fell in love with Campanini, and as naturally fell out again as soon as Mr. Hammerstein found it possible to do without him. But apparently it took six conductors to fill his place. He has since gone over to the enemy and taken charge of the branch Metropolitan establishment just formed at Chicago.

So far the Manhattan enterprise has done comparatively little for the native singer, beyond granting facilities for experience in small parts and the chorus. I remember suggesting to Mr. Hammerstein during his first season the advisability of producing an American opera. He simply laughed. He has recently thought better of it, and commissioned Mr. Victor Herbert and Mr. Reginald de Koven to write grand operas

for him ; but at that time he did not believe
at all in American operas and not very much
in American singers.

I warned him against restricting himself
exclusively to the Italian répertoire, old or
modern.*   He grew serious, and vowed that
he would fight Conried and Ricordi for his
promised share of the Puccini operas.   He
did, too, and won !

Subsequently, I pointed out to him that
there was one operatic field which in New
York was comparatively untouched—namely,
the modern French.   A significant smile came
slowly over Mr. Hammerstein's face.   He
asked me if I had ever heard Mary Garden.
I replied that I had.

"Well," he said, after a pause, "if I could
get Mary Garden at a reasonable figure I
would do the new French operas in which

---

* Being of an obstinate as well as sanguine disposition,
Mr. Hammerstein embarked upon a preliminary season of Italian
Opera at cheap prices, just prior to his regular season of 1909–10.
It resulted in a heavy loss.   Had he tried opera in English for a
change, he might have lost less money and conferred a direct
benefit upon American singers.

she has made a hit, and take my chance of
her making a success in New York."

I observed that he would have to mount
"Pelléas et Melisande" and engage French
artists to support the untried Chicago singer.
"I would do all that," he replied, "if I could
get Mary Garden." Then I made him a proposition. I told him I thought I could help
him to secure her through the late Mr. Gustave
Schirmer (of the New York publishing firm)
and Mr. Durand, the Paris publisher of
"Pelléas." Mr. Hammerstein said, "Go
ahead."

I did so. Mr. Schirmer, who unfortunately
did not live to see the result of his efforts,
began the negotiations, and succeeded so well
that the Manhattan impresario, when he went
to Paris that summer, found the ground
perfectly laid for a contract.

Such was the beginning of the Mary Garden
episode, perhaps the most remarkable, certainly the most entertaining, feature of Oscar
Hammerstein's enterprise down to date. It
was a case of taking possession of the public

from the outset, and that in the teeth of a
determined opposition on the part of most
of the critics.

Is the condition of opera in America any
healthier for the vogue of a Mary Garden ?
. . . It certainly has given New York the new
French operas ; and that is not a smaller
achievement in its way than the introduction
of the Puccini operas at the Metropolitan.
But it has hardly compensated for the total
exclusion of the German masterpieces from
the stage of the Manhattan.

The triumph of Luisa Tetrazzini, in the
same season (1907–8) that Mary Garden
made her *début*, added immensely to the *éclat*
of the undertaking, and incidentally diverted
a large amount of cash from the coffers of the
Metropolitan Opera House. The success of
these two prima donnas fairly established upon
a safe operatic pinnacle the energetic Mr.
Hammerstein, who thereupon erected new
opera-houses in Philadelphia and Brooklyn
and extended his labours to Boston, Baltimore,
and other places.

Since then the American people have literally gone "opera-mad." They are now spending thousands of dollars on opera where they formerly spent hundreds. The prices of opera singers have gone up fifty per cent. The troupes and the répertoires are of prodigious size. Every large city is hungry to emulate New York's example and possess its own operatic establishment. Where will it end?

Gatti-Casazza and Dippel

I have already said that the phenomenal success of the Manhattan experiment brought the directors of the Metropolitan to a timely sense of the necessities of their position. They felt the support of the two and three-dollar public slipping away from them, though fortunately the subscription more than remained intact. Nothing could be done, however, until the moment came for choosing a successor to Mr. Conried. They then proceeded to act with a supreme disregard for the teachings of experience and common sense.

How it all came about is no mystery. But the story is too long to tell in these pages ; and besides, a game of wire-pulling, wherein every conceivable move is executed with the subtlety and finesse peculiar to American elections, does not make either novel or edifying reading. Suffice it to say that in the end the Metropolitan found itself landed with two *impresarii* instead of one.

The new general manager, Signor Giulio Gatti-Casazza and the new administrative manager, Herr Andreas Dippel, notwithstanding their distinctive titles, practically share the same post. One is at the head of affairs, the other very nearly so ; and they agree to display so much unanimity of opinion and action as it is within reason to expect from men of diametrically opposite training and traditions.

It is not anticipated that this dual form of government—now in its third season—will be permanently maintained. It may also be doubted whether the combination has tended to enhance the prosperity of this institution from a financial point of view, though one gladly recognizes that in an artistic sense many faults have been remedied. The presence of a common danger has led to a good many improvements ; and, thanks to the unlimited resources placed at their disposal by a board of millionaires, the two directors have been able to indulge in a lavish extravagance of outlay for artists and *mise en scène* the like of which has never seen a parallel in operatic history.

Such is the present aspect of the famous "opera war" in New York. The struggle has now entered upon its fourth "round," and to all appearance has only just begun. Both sides have strengthened their positions by extending their fields of labour to the more important cities within reach. As a consequence they can afford to engage enormous companies, to produce eight or ten novelties in a season, and to give not only simultaneous performances, but sometimes four in a day

(two matinée and two evening), in opera
houses a couple of hundred miles apart.

Is it the apotheosis of the star that we
are witnessing in this tremendous display of
activity ?   Or will the Gargantuan feast in
which the American public is now revelling
create an appetite of the kind that "grows
by what it feeds upon," and, instead of producing satiety, engender a real, deep, abiding
and unalterable love of opera for its own
sake—opera well given but no longer dependent upon the all-pervading personality of the
star ?

Or, again, is there a chance that on the crest
of such a tidal wave opera sung in English and
opera by American composers—the "Flotsam
and Jetson" of the lyric stage—will be borne
into a benign and hospitable harbour ?   As
these lines are penned there is indeed some
slight—but, alas ! very slight—promise of actual
fulfilment in this important matter.

Herein London has so far led the way, but
seems to have stopped short at the *crux* of the

movement. Were New York now to take this up and carry it to a triumphant issue, it would be credited with a noble reform and earn thereby the right to be called, where Opera is concerned, a typically " musical city."

VIII.—GENII OF THE CONCERT WORLD

THE genii of the "Arabian Nights," as most people are aware, were a class of beings gifted with supernatural powers, which they were credited with exercising sometimes for beneficent, sometimes for evil purposes, but always with the ultimate view of pointing a moral to the tale.

The musical genii of New York have nothing of the supernatural in their make-up ; neither do I wish for a moment to suggest that they include the wayward specimens whose disposition is of the maleficent order. But they are genii for all that, because it is they who shape the course of musical events, and it is in their hands that the fate of so many personages in the story actually rests.

In the cosmos of the concert world these genii are not numerous, but they are powerful. Their labours are more or less clearly defined, they do not interfere with one another, and the wonder of their achievement lies in this : that they direct and carry on with smoothness, if not success, concert institutions which, in the strict commercial sense, do not pay their way.

To explain. The quantity of good music performed in New York is, as has already been shown, stupendous. Who supports it ? If the answer to that question could be given in a word—" the public," then the title of this book, with or without its note of interrogation, would have no *raison d'être*. But it cannot ; for the simple reason that if the magnificent orchestral undertakings which are the main feature and the pride of New York musical life had to depend solely upon the people who subscribe for seats or pay at the doors, they could not possibly go on.

Who makes up the losses ?

This is where the adroitness of the genii

comes in.   Apart from the work of administration, theirs is the task of calling upon millionaires
and wealthy amateurs and securing the financial
aid, in the shape either of substantial dona-
tions or guarantees, wherewith to furnish the
necessary reserve funds for making good the
deficits.   It may be a delicate task, but it is
not an unpleasant one.   For notwithstanding the
heavy claims upon their purses, rich men and
women in New York are apt to be generous
in the support of their prominent musical
institutions ; at any rate some of them are ;
and I am told that the persuasive powers of
the genii are irresistible.

It comes to this, then : It is not the many,
but the few—not the general body of the
community, but a limited section of the interested musical public—that supplies the large
guarantee funds without which these leading
concert enterprises would come to a stand-
still.

Let us by all means admire the city that
can yield such valuable resources ; but let us
not mistake the real artistic conditions, nor

imagine that they have changed so very much since the days when the great musicians had to rely wholly upon their princes and archbishops and archdukes for the lucrative pursuit of their art.

Oratorio seems to be going out of fashion in other countries besides England. In New York its decline would appear to have progressed in inverse ratio to the spread of the opera fever. But just as choral music in the English provinces is more popular than in the British capital, so does it create far more interest in Boston and Chicago and Festival centres like Worcester and Cincinnati than in the Empire City.

Thus, the Oratorio Society of New York stands in circumstances almost identical with those which govern our Royal Albert Hall Choral Society, in that both derive their principal income from their annual performances of the " Messiah." Only the English society, having the much larger locale, contents itself with one " Messiah " concert ; whereas the

American always contrives to fill Carnegie Hall twice during the week intervening between Christmas and New Year's Day. Even at these, however, the average attendance has sensibly decreased in recent years.

Two other prominent societies, the Musical Art Society and the People's Choral Union, do useful work in their respective domains—the former giving *a cappella* and other difficult compositions ; the latter well-known oratorios, for which low prices of admission are charged.

It is a distinct disadvantage, however, that these three choral bodies should all be under the same conductor. He may be a good genie, but being human, it is not in his power to accomplish for three organizations what he could for one. There is a too consistent sameness of policy ; many more rehearsals might be held ; and if the operations of the three societies do not clash (because they do not cover quite the same ground), so much the worse for the healthy condition of choral music in New York.

One misses altogether there the spirit of

emulation evoked by the efforts of rival choirs, by the keen struggles for supremacy between bodies of voices of similar size and calibre. There are more of such competitions in the little Principality of Wales than in the whole of the United States. Yet experience has shown it to be the element that can best imbue with fresh life and attraction a department of music in which public interest gives indication of becoming more and more sluggish.

It is of vital importance, this continued prosperity of choral enterprise, to the development of music as a national art in America. These concerts employ the native soloist more than any others. They bring musicians, students, amateurs, and auditors to the same arena to take part in and listen to the masterpieces of three centuries. Their educational value is inestimable. They afford the native composer infinitely better opportunities for a hearing (and a livelihood) than the opera houses, with all their wealth of popularity and enterprise.

For the cost of a new opera twenty new choral works can be produced. How often does either appear on a New York bill with the name of an American musician under it? —the former once in many years, the latter as an occasional but rare occurrence. And why?

Because until quite recently the names of MacDowell, Parker, Chadwick, Converse, and others have been neither familiar nor acceptable to the paying public of New York. To print those names to-day on the posters outside Carnegie Hall may not be to court disaster as it would have done at one time, but it is still an unprofitable and possibly expensive proceeding.

Maybe New York will gradually assume a kinder attitude towards choral music and the Americans who write it. Meanwhile every contribution to the guarantee funds of the choral societies should be given on the understanding that room be made in each season's programme for a certain proportion of novelties by native composers.

Orchestral concerts constitute, after Opera, the most favoured form of musical entertainment on the New York list. It has been so since the days of Theodore Thomas, Leopold Damrosch, and Anton Seidl. To say that the orchestra is flourishing more vigorously than ever as we enter upon the second decade of the twentieth century, is to give but a feeble idea of the extent to which it has stimulated the imagination and caught the fancy of this music-ridden population.

Thanks to the energy of the genii and the liberality of the guarantors and donors of ever-swelling funds, the two leading local institutions—the Philharmonic and the New York Symphony Societies—stand at this moment upon a remarkably elevated plane of prosperity. Both have quite lately been re-organized and now possess permanent salaried orchestras, one directed by Gustav Mahler, the other by Walter Damrosch. Their rivalry cannot fail to prove beneficial.

Superior to either is the famous Boston Symphony Orchestra, which has given an

annual series of concerts in New York since
1887. Albeit a subsidized body, the Boston
players are now very nearly self-supporting,
and I have been told that their visits to New
York almost always yield a profit. The fact
is creditable alike to the orchestra and to
the city: and doubly so because this superb
organization borrows less than any other of
its rank in America from the brilliancy of a
" star " conductor.

In addition to the above, there are the
concerts given by the Russian Symphony Society
and the Volpe Orchestra, both largely sustained by private subscriptions. Also the
admirable People's Symphony Concerts, ex-
pressly intended to improve and cultivate the
taste of the humblest music lovers ; and the
Young People's Symphony Concerts, which perform a similar instructive function for juvenile
amateurs. These are supported as philanthropic
or educational institutions. Furthermore, there
is an orchestra conducted by Victor Herbert,
and yet another which performs symphonic
works under the direction of Manuel Klein.

With such an enormous aggregate, it will be guessed that the supply of orchestral concerts is terribly in excess of the demand. Unlike opera, they awaken no responsive chord in the hearts of the people. Certainly the multitude prefer Sousa and the "rag-time" bands, which never appeal in vain when they put forward their popular selections, including plenty of marches and waltzes, on a Sunday evening.

Truth to tell, the orchestral situation in New York is in a state of transition. There is much thorough and sincere appreciation of the best that is to be heard in serious music. The classical masterpieces are beloved and fine orchestral playing is intensely enjoyed.

At the same time the adorers of Beethoven seem to find little attraction in ultra-modern works ; and, *vice versâ*, the admirers of the young German and French schools too often confess themselves bored by the old masters. Without the co-operation of the star-conductor, the star-vocalist, or the star-instrumentalist, most of these orchestras would fare badly. The genuine connoisseur studies the programme as a whole, but with the ordinary amateur it is the name in big letters that turns the scale.

When the rising generation knows its own mind better, when a more solid eclectic taste prevails, and when the administration and working of orchestral institutions are less coloured by the influence of the social genie, then conditions in this important branch will be more satisfactory than they are at present.

The remaining features of New York concert life I may dismiss very briefly.

Of chamber music there is a superabundance —again not in proportion to the extent of the musical population, but as measured by its capacity for absorbing this most elevated and refined form of abstract music.   With the exception of the Kneisel Quartet (which has taken nearly twenty years to establish itself as a self-supporting concern), not a single organization of the kind can claim to be able to make an annual series of chamber concerts pay in New York.

There must be at least a round dozen of quartet parties and trios giving concerts frequently at Mendelssohn Hall and in the hotel *salons*. Most of them consist of excellent players, but without the support of personal friends they would never cover their expenses. Luckily, they are not disappointed if they do not. In most cases it is purely for the New York advertisement that they are working. Whatever they may earn there as teachers, it is from outside that the performers derive their living — from the splendid Women's Clubs and well-managed musical societies that abound in the states of New York, New Jersey, Connecticut, Rhode Island, Massachusets and Maine.

The good genie of chamber music revealed himself a few years ago in Mr. E. J. de Coppet, a distinguished lover and wealthy patron of the art, who set a splendid example by defraying the entire expense of training and bringing out the Flonzaley Quartet. These fine artists have since won a European reputation, and now stand only second to the Kneisels

in public favour.   Next to them come the
Olive Mead Quartet, the Maud Powell Trio
and the Margulies Trio.

But really only a tiny percentage of New
York amateurs care a rap for chamber music.
I tested the point pretty conclusively myself at
the "Sunday Pops," to which reference has
already been made.   I even tried the experiment of abbreviating (much against my inclina-
tion) the noblest quartets and sonatas of
Mozart, Haydn, Beethoven, Schubert, Schumann, and Brahms, thinking that one or two
movements from each might prove more
digestible than the whole.   The idea seemed
acceptable to those who came ; but it did not
help to draw larger audiences.

It is, I think, beyond dispute that the form
of concert which most attracts the musically-
inclined section of this community is the
recital given at Carnegie Hall by the solitary
star of the voice, the piano, or the violin.
Here one may count upon finding the biggest
crowds, the biggest receipts (or, rather, profits),
and the biggest displays of enthusiasm.

But there are only a round dozen artists in all the world capable of achieving this triumph single-handed. They comprise Marcella Sembrich, Ernestine Schumann - Heink, Lillian Nordica, Emma Eames, Johanna Gadski, and David Bispham, among vocalists ; Paderewski, Moriz Rosenthal, and Fanny Bloomfield-Zeisler, among pianists ; Ysaye, Kreisler, and Kubelik, among violinists. N.B.—Four of these are born Americans.

Once in a way the feat may be sucessfully attempted by some new but highly-renowned visitor — a Saint-Saëns, for example, or a Chaminade. But this is quite the exception. For the ordinary singer or instrumentalist, coming from Europe unheralded or minus "sensation," New York can be counted upon to furnish the coldest of cold *douches*.

Money, of course, will purchase an appearance at a Mendelssohn Hall recital or a *début* of some sort through the medium of an influential musical agent. As a rule, however, the agent will not take an unknown artist under his wing unless a premium be paid ;

and that may cost anything from a thousand to two thousand dollars. Then there is the necessary advertising in the local daily and musical journals, a very expensive item. Hence may the *débutant* visiting New York in search of fame and fortune, instead of making money, be saddled with an outlay of from two to four or even five thousand dollars. *Verbum sap.**

The New York concert agent belongs to a growing tribe of genii, whose power and sphere of influence are broadening with the daily increase in the gigantic ramifications of American musical enterprise.

When the late Henry Wolfsohn entered this field, a quarter of a century ago, he had it well-nigh to himself. He ploughed it so profitably that by the time he quitted it [his death occurred in the spring of 1909] the number of first-class " Musical Bureaux " in New York

* These figures are in no sense exaggerated. They only depend upon the depth of the artist's pocket and a corresponding determination to persevere until the real verdict of the public (and the critics) has been ascertained.

alone had mounted up to to ten or twelve.
There are now a few in other cities ; but their
operations are chiefly restricted to their own
sections, whereas from this great centre the
industrious concert-manager extends his con-
necting links over the entire Union.

And he is a real genie, is this example of
the species. (Do not confound him with the
fakir, whose tricks are illusory and valueless at
best.) Give him the material—it must be something besides mere cash, since America pays
for genuine talent alone—and you shall see
what marvels he will accomplish.

He knows everybody. It is his duty to be
acquainted with every concert *entrepreneur*,
every choral or orchestral conductor, every
leading organist, every president of a musical
society or glee union or women's club, *et hoc
genus omne*, from New York to San Francisco,
from New Orleans to Canada. He must be
able (and he can, if the conditions be right) to
effect engagements as the seasons come round
with any or all of these people, whom he calls
upon in person, at distances ranging from a

couple of hundred to two thousand miles, when he is organizing tours for his clients.

His terms vary.   The star considers him cheap ; the established artist thinks him worth while ; the *débutant* finds him dear : but to all alike he is indispensable.   In most cases he works for a commission.   There are instances, albeit rare, where he is something of a capitalist, engaging his artists by contract and letting them out at a profit.   Under all circumstances he makes money.

He deserves to, for he works hard ; and, generally speaking, this genie is honest.   It is to his interest to satisfy both sides of his *clientèle*, and the task is often a delicate one.

A simple piece of luck can make his fortune. I met with an instance of this whilst arranging my " Sunday Pops."   It was, of course, the exploitation of a " sensation " ; and I only just escaped the felicity of being the introducer thereof.

One morning a concert agent, whom I had never seen or heard of before, called upon me and offered to secure for me Dr. Ludwig

Wüllner, the well-known German interpreter of Lieder, who was about to undertake his first tour in America. Having heard Dr. Wüllner in London, I said I should be glad to engage him, if possible, for my opening concert.

The terms, in arranging which the agent showed himself most considerate, were ultimately agreed upon, and the matter of the date was left open. But at a subsequent interview a serious point arose. Dr. Wüllner's manager informed me that it would be essential for his principal to monopolize the entire programme. This, I informed him, was contrary to the published scheme of my concerts. The idea was to bring first-rate artists into co-operation, not to exploit isolated stars.

Thus the engagement fell through. But during the same autumn Dr. Wüllner made his *début* at Mendelssohn Hall and achieved one of those extraordinary successes—easier, perhaps, to understand than to explain—that from time to time electrify New York. In that one season the artist pocketed more money than he

H

had made in Europe during the preceding five years. The agent laid the foundation of a large business, and has since taken his place among the prominent concert-managers of the country.

IX.—MUSIC IN THE CHURCHES

I ONCE heard this colloquy :
  " What church do you go to ? "
  " St. ———."
      " Dear me ! Surely you don't go there
for the preacher ? "

" No, indeed. I go for the music. It's the
best in New York."

Music in American churches serves a twofold
purpose. It heightens the beauty of the service
and helps to attract a larger congregation.
Incidentally it affords useful and often lucrative
employment to singers, not only providing a
substantial " nest-egg " for their regular income,
but assisting them in many cases to pay for the
completion of their musical training.

With scarcely an exception, every prima
donna of American birth on the operatic stage
has begun her career as a vocalist and earned

her first few dollars by singing in the choir of some church. For as a rule the choir in American churches does not consist of boys, but of a quartet of male and female soloists, sometimes supported by a small body of mixed voices.

The system, therefore, is beneficial in more senses than one, and calls for commendation no less than encouragement. It will deserve a large meed of both as long as it continues to maintain the high standard heretofore associated with it.

Certain of the New York churches have long been famous for the quality of their music. Among them there is keen competition for the services of the first-rate solo singers. They pay high salaries. A fine soprano can command from 1000 dols. to 2500 dols. per annum ; and in one notable instance, where there is but a single soloist, a popular oratorio soprano receives as much as 3000 dols. for singing on thirty Sundays in the year.

Naturally there are plenty of applicants for these posts whenever a vacancy occurs. Not

long ago a new bass soloist was required at
St. Bartholomew's Church; the position was
kept open for several months, and over two
hundred candidates were tried before a selection
was finally made.

The preliminary tests are conducted by the
organist, but the ultimate decision rests with
the Music Committee of the church, aided,
perhaps, by the pastor himself. These gentlemen are generally innocent of musical training;
but, inasmuch as the more promising of the
selected candidates are permitted to sing at a
trial service, their choice is doubtless somewhat
influenced by the opinions of their wives or
relatives. In the end, therefore, few complaints
are heard.

Unfortunately it is the custom, save in
exceptional cases, to limit the contracts to one
year only. At some churches, indeed, there
is a change in the constitution of the quartet
as regularly as the twelve months come round.
This constant " coming and going " engenders
an atmosphere of uncertainty, and the conse-
quent variations in the *personnel* of the quartet

are unquestionably detrimental to the stability and polish of the *ensemble*.

There are other peculiarities connected with this church work which, I am bound to say, are not calculated to elevate the artistic ideas of the singer.

In certain churches a sufficiently high standard is observed. The music is carefully selected, and on special occasions cantatas by well-known writers and portions of the familiar oratorios are creditably performed. But these form the minority.

At most churches the music includes a large proportion of " sacred songs " of an *ad captandum* type—spurious imitations of the Mendelssohn-Gounod style, by writers of the *Kapellmeistermusik* order, who make an excellent living out of their suavely effective effusions. These " pot-boilers " are little if aught superior to the much-derided British ballad ; but they are supposed to please audiences to whom music of a higher class would not make the same appeal.

The soloist who is required to sing this

dull, pretentious stuff deserves to be pitied. Nor can the blame be laid altogether at the door of the organist. If he be a "strong man" and in a position to put his foot down, his feeling as a trained musician and his natural love for the artistic will assert themselves to the extent of keeping the sacred pot-boiler out of the service. On the other hand, he is too frequently obliged to cater to the whims and fancies of his committee or congregation.

Thus it is that the mixture of styles presented by New York church music is at times so inconceivably quaint as to make a theatre or restaurant programme look positively consistent by comparison.

Obviously the moral to be deduced from all this is that the interference of the layman should forthwith cease. Or, at least, if it be advisable for him to continue to have the last word in the choice of soloists, his particular taste, or that of his family, should not be allowed to dictate in the slightest degree the character of the solo anthem. The question of the latter would then, as an American would say, be " up to " the organist.

The worst of it is that the exact authority of the organist is not clearly defined ; it differs in the various churches almost as much as does that of the conductors in the opera houses. In one he is " lord of all he surveys ; " there the music will be admirable.   In another he is at the beck and call of the committee and the humble servant of the vicar ; chaos accordingly.

The organist ought to have the right, not merely to choose every note that is sung, but to veto any piece that he does not consider up to the requisite high level.   It may be that he does technically possess that right in the majority of the places of worship.   If so, it is to be regretted that he does not enforce it more frequently, and with less regard for the inferior musical taste of the people who govern and support his church.

In one respect alone would I desire to check the power of the organist, and that is when he presumes to interfere with the voices of his choristers and teach them how to sing. He is *ex officio* the trainer of his choir, but not their individual voice-trainer. He probably knows nothing whatever about the art of singing ; consequently when dissatisfied with some feature appertaining thereto, his duty is to refer the vocalist to his or her teacher. His attempts at personal instruction will in all probability lead to worse results.

More than one such case of unwarrantable interference with the singer on a point of technique came under my own notice whilst I was in New York. In every instance I requested my pupil not to acknowledge the right of the organist to do more than offer a frank criticism of the supposed fault.

Take them for all in all, though, the New York organists are a splendid set of musicians —capable, industrious, conscientious, and thorough. Many of them, too, are executants of a superior order, whose recitals are well worth attending and of real educative value.

It is quite in the power of such men to

uphold the best traditions of music in their churches. They should see to it that no minor considerations, no petty desire to gratify an ignoble or vulgar taste, be permitted to lower by a single notch the exalted standard of the school in which they themselves were reared.

X.—THE COURSE OF MUSICAL CULTURE

"**S**TORY ? God bless you, sir, I've none to tell ! "

System ?—New York's system of musical education ?—dear reader, the thing does not exist !

With all its flood of operas and concerts and exhibitions of matured talent, the Empire City yet lacks the one essential for creating within itself a recognized source of musical learning, a definite arbiter of musical taste, a true fountain-head from which to instil and refresh the spirit of musical appreciation.

In other words, it has no great central institution, either national or municipal, which stands in the same relation to the people of New York—or for that matter the United States—that the Conservatoire de Musique does to Paris, the Hochschule to Berlin, the Royal Academy or the Royal College of Music to London.

I am not sure whether the importance of such an institution, or rather, the effect of its absence, is rightly grasped. To understand it, then, imagine what a country full of *soi-disant* colleges and technical schools would be in this age without a university. Oh yes, you are " a young country," I know ! I have often heard so. But your young country already possesses more universities, and richer ones, than England, France, and Germany put together !

You ask, perhaps, " Does this Conservatoire or Academy or Hochschule bear the same relation to Music that Yale or Harvard, Oxford or Cambridge, bears to the national pursuit of knowledge in all its more exalted forms ? " If so, why do these same universities include the study and higher development of musical art in their own curriculum, and appoint a Professor to a lucrative Chair of Music for the purpose of superintending it ?

The reply to the first question is a simple

"Yes." To the second it may be answered that musical study in the universities is, or should be, with the object of obtaining degrees, to confer which is likewise the principal purpose of the university's inclusion of music within its sphere of activity. The university cannot take the place of the college or high school ; neither could the latter perform their functions with entire efficiency were their standards and methods not so modelled upon those of the university as to make them the natural stepping stone to the higher institution.

It is a great intermediate institution of this description that Paris has in its Conservatoire, Berlin in its Hochschule, London in its Royal Academy and Royal College.* But they are not necessarily stepping - stones to the university. They are themselves finishing schools of music. They do not admit beginners. They require proof of talent and elementary training. They

---

* I am aware that these institutions are not beyond criticism. Each in certain departments leaves something to be desired. But they constitute the centres of a great and indispensable educational force, whence method and standard spontaneously spring.

do not depend upon fees alone. They receive State support and they own property and endowments which they can bestow upon their students in the form of scholarships and free education in every branch of the art.

Nay, more. They have their orchestras, their opera-classes, their public performances, which not alone give constant opportunities for practice, but furnish an additional and more effective medium than any other for spreading their educational influence among the masses— yes, literally among the humblest of the respectable ranks of the population, since their students are drawn from every section of the community.

Above all they have their valuable system of examinations. This, in the case of the two London institutions, is carried on by an "Associated Board," which sends its representative examiners from end to end of the United Kingdom and to every part of the British Dominions beyond the seas. Every "outside" student of music is at liberty to become a candidate at these examinations ; and thus, besides setting the much-needed standard, they bring the entire musical population of the empire into actual touch with a common Alma Mater.

I cannot but think that the lack of an institution such as this, together with the more or less systematic and definite course of musical education which would follow in its wake, is largely responsible for the limited amount of true artistic culture and genuine refinement of musical taste that one perceives even among the better classes in New York. Who can follow properly when nobody—or everybody—takes the lead ?

New Yorkers—let me say it again—are intensely fond of good music. Like all Americans, they have a quick ear ; they enjoy a real melody ; they appreciate fine orchestral or solo playing ; and they recognize as readily as any other public the characteristics of good vocal tone and good singing. Most of these qualities account for their special love of opera, which they may be said, indeed, to have " in their blood."

But mere delight in sensuous musical charm, or even love of the pure and beautiful in music, does not suffice for the complete understanding of a great master's inspired ideas, or for plumbing the depths of the emotions that his music is intended to express. The capacity for this lies in early training, in environment, in the habit of studying and listening to classical masterpieces, in the influence of teachers and fellow-students who have acquired their thoughts and methods at some undefiled and authoritative source.

It does not suffice to follow symphonies with the aid of books or primers that instruct the credulous amateur " how to listen." Still less does it suffice to criticize strange music-dramas through the preliminary experience of lectures, at which the various "leitmotives" are carefully but ineffectively executed upon a pianoforte. There are more " musical guides " published in New York than in any other city I know ; but their practical worth, which I have tested in every possible way, is absolutely disappointing.

More benefit by far will accrue in course of

time from the concerts for juveniles, at which the movements or " programmes " of the various works are orally explained. These audiences are youthful, and therefore at an age to learn. But it is not by dint of mere listening nor by the simultaneous perusal of more or less academic " explanatory notes " that adults, however keen their love of music, can hope to comprehend the mysteries of the " sonata form," to analyze the secrets and devices of modern orchestration, to follow the sempiternal modulations of a Debussy or a Reger, and to grasp the elusive significance of a work based upon a structure of metaphysical ideas or profound poetic sentiment.

We judge a man by what he professes to do or be able to do. In similar fashion ought we to judge a country or a community.

Now, New York professes—through the mouths or pens of those who consider themselves entitled to speak in its behalf—to have, to be, and to do practically everything. There is, I admit, a good deal of ground for this assumption, in regard to music as well as other things. But it would be futile to attempt to prove that there exists any teaching establishment in that city which either serves, or could be made to serve, as a satisfactory substitute for such a central musical institution as I have above described.

Schools of music there are, proclaiming lofty ambitions and bearing pretentious titles. Their utility, however, is strictly limited to their teaching capacity, whatever that may be. One may do better work than another ; but none possesses the authority or has yet demonstrated the ability to set up a general standard that can compare with the standard of the European Conservatoires.

Where there is no standard there can be no system ; and without system the process of musical education and culture can at best be but a haphazard affair. Now, although it has not a single great teaching institution, New York counts its teachers by the thousand. It could do no doubt the same, were it practicable, with the young people who go thither every year from all parts of the Union for the sole purpose of studying music, professionally or otherwise.

To what a terrible extent must the element of chance enter into their choice of a professor ! Name or reputation may guide them in some degree ; but even that, as experience is constantly proving, may turn out a delusion and a snare.

One notoriously bad outcome of present conditions in this respect is that students, whether from without or within, stay but a comparatively short period under the same teacher. They indulge in the meretricious habit of flitting from studio to studio to see what crumbs of information and knowledge they can pick up from different masters. The natural result is that they absorb opposing ideas and adopt a variety of methods which either leave them minus a definite style or, more frequently still, with a vicious one.

How can it be otherwise, when no recognized standard or test of efficiency is applied to the work of the teachers, and when there is no system of examinations by which the actual merit of the students can be ascertained ?

It is true that in recent years the teachers have formed associations of their own, and some of these are now doing excellent service, alike by improving the pedagogic art and by training advanced students to become members of their profession. They realize the importance of interchanging ideas and holding discussions concerning the problems or knotty points of their occupation. They begin to perceive that an amalgamation of interests can achieve more for the general weal than any amount of individual striving.

So far the instrumental teachers have met with greater success in this direction than the teachers of singing. The latter founded a " National Association " some five or six years ago, which at one time gave promise of initiating and accomplishing valuable reforms for the protection of the public and for the advantage of the profession generally. Of that association I saw a great deal, since for nearly three years I acted as chairman of its

Executive Board and resigned only a few weeks before returning to England, namely in June, 1909.

The notion that singing teachers can get together and agree upon a broad definition of the technical principles of their art is universally discredited. Strange to say, the National Association did accomplish this remarkable feat, and the rock upon which we split was not a matter of mechanism but a question of policy.

I held (and the majority of members agreed with me) that the first duty of the association was to examine candidates as to their fitness and ability to teach singing, and if satisfactory, to award them diplomas. The minority were of opinion that there ought not to be examinations, and that the first thing to do was to establish a school for the training of vocal teachers.

Upon the horns of this dilemma member after member of the executive board resigned, and the whole organization threatened to tumble to pieces. I appealed to the leader of the minority, but he remained implacable. Then, to prevent further disruption and knowing that I was soon to leave New York, I tendered my own resignation, and with much regret said good-bye to the National Association of Teachers of Singing.

Thus ended a dream of unity and good-fellowship which many declared at the time to be Utopian, but which, had it not been for the stubbornness (if nothing else) of the individual referred to, would unquestionably have been realized.

Nevertheless co-operative action for the amelioration of the professional musician's status in New York is bound to come sooner or later ; and the singing teachers need it more than any other branch, for theirs is the least healthy.   Their ranks are overgrown with charlatans and humbugs whose incapacity is only exceeded by their assurance and impudence.

It is the positive physical injury wrought upon their pupils' throats and chests through unskilful manipulation by these ignorant and

shameless impostors that has in turn reflected
so seriously upon the reputation for ability
of the vocal teachers as a body.   Indeed, I
may add in parenthesis that during my long
residence in New York I found that what
is termed " Society " looked down upon music
teachers of every class with undisguised
contempt.

Meanwhile the trouble is that the public
has no reliable guide to enable it to distinguish
good teachers from bad.   The schools include
specimens of both, so that even they cannot
be wholly trusted—a state of affairs which,
so far as vocal instruction is concerned,
certainly prevails in other cities, European
and American, besides New York.

Many of the teachers are still indirectly
responsible for the preference shown by the
younger generation for music of the lightest
and most trivial description.   Happily this
sin is growing less universal ; and in a great
many instances it is the fault of parents whose
musical taste does not soar beyond common-
place tunes and " fireworks."   Anyhow, the

teachers are either held back in this regard by indifference, or by the fear of losing their pupils through asking them to swallow what their palates do not relish.

On an average one hears better music from the graphophone—for example the operatic airs sung by world-famous artists—than the inane pieces that are constantly being drummed upon the piano within the hallowed precincts of the domestic " parlor."

Is it surprising, then (to revert in conclusion to an old story), when one finds the concert-rooms, especially at recitals, sheltering a larger proportion of " dead-heads " than in London, where seats are more expensive and where there are twice or even three times as many concerts taking place as in New York ? Is it surprising to find the young people devoting their spare pocket-money, not to the enjoyment of high-class music, but to the variety theatres and the cinematograph shows ?

And finally, when we search among the avowed music-lovers, where intelligent appreciation is supposed to dominate, is it surprising to find the characteristic craving for the sensational taking first place, and relegating purer and nobler artistic considerations to the background ?

XI.—MUSICAL CRITICISM : THE REAL AND THE IDEAL

I NOW approach the closing and in some respects most difficult portion of my task. The subject of newspaper criticism is always a delicate one, and should be handled only with kid gloves. Well, I figuratively put those gloves on—not in a sarcastic spirit, as Wagner did when he was about to conduct the Mendelssohn piece ; nor with a sense of fear, for I know neither " fear nor favour " in writing this book.

No : simply because I desire to avoid giving offence to those who have never offended me, and because I wish above all things to prevent the slightest suspicion of being actuated by a personal motive. Once more, I have no axe to grind, no grudge to repay—but I must not protest further. Some one will be crying, *Qui s'excuse, s'accuse !*

If I claim to speak impartially on the subject of musical criticism in New York, I can also claim to do so with a pretty accurate knowledge of its idiosyncracies. I knew the critics themselves intimately ; I read them assiduously ; and, during the first year I lived there, I myself wrote many articles on the opera and other musical subjects for the *New York Herald.* This may, I think, be fairly said to constitute what the French call *connaissance de cause.*

There is no group of musical journalists more intensely feared than those who write for the New York papers. Some, of course, are more feared than others ; one, perhaps, most of all. In the aggregate they excite in the minds of the artist a degree of trepidation that can best be likened to what must have been felt by the ancient Greeks when waiting the periodical deliverances of their most redoubtable oracles.

I did not need to go to America to learn

this fact.   Twenty years ago the tenor Alvary
(then already a New York favourite) made his
début at Covent Garden, and on the night of
his first appearance I met him on the stage just
before the curtain went up.   He was looking
the very picture of nervous anxiety.

"What is the matter?" I asked.   "Anything wrong with your voice?"

"Nothing," he replied.   "It was never
better.   I am only wondering what dreadful
holes you critics will find to pick in me.   Are
you as bad as the New York critics?"

"I am not sure.   I think not.   But what
makes you ask?"

"Only this," said poor Alvary.   "They
have no mercy when they have not yet heard
you.   Once they know what you can do, it's
all right; till then they show you no pity!"

Here is the whole matter in a nutshell.

I once asked an English singer—he, too,
was a tenor and a famous one—on his return
from a long tour in the States, what he had to
say about the American musical critics.   Like
a shot came the counter-question—

"Which do you mean—the New York critics or the others ? "

" I mean the critics as a body.   But why the distinction ? "

" Because there is a great one.   In New York if they don't admire you they ' roast ' you ; and if you displease them they flay you alive.   In Boston, Chicago, and the other places they also seem to understand what they are writing about ; but they are not so cruel, and they are more fair because they give you full credit for whatever they do like."

This reputation for severity the New York critics are positively proud of.   They have won it by hard fighting and they mean apparently to retain it.   It has some advantages.   It keeps out the "incapables."   It gives the world to understand that there is no room in their city for any but the best. It keeps the musician up to the mark and the amateur on the *qui vive*.   By arousing fear and apprehension in the one it creates an impression of mysterious power in the other.   An attitude of lofty superiority, supported by a sufficient display of knowledge, cannot fail to enhance the dignity and importance of any critic.

Towards new-comers, unfortunately, it is almost an attitude of menace.   It betokens generally a harsh and threatening frame of mind rather than a considerate and judicial one.*   Not infrequently it reveals itself in language that is by turns satirical and cajoling, caustic and contemptuous.   I have even known it condescend to abuse.   But its purpose is at least never doubtful, and that is one good point.

Again, the attitude of extreme severity is not reserved for foreigners ; it is manifested with equal impartiality towards born Americans. The effect is more serious, however, upon the former than upon the latter.

The *débutant* from abroad suffers palpably

---

* There are, I am glad to say, one or two exceptions to this rule, but I must not be indiscreet enough to name them.   The trouble in these cases is that it seems so hard for the critics to find the *juste milieu* between excessive admiration and utter dislike.

and directly through a strongly adverse criticism ; the discouragement is so great that
recovery from it is probably out of the
question. The native artist may feel discouraged too, but knows the conditions better,
and, instead of sitting down under the lash,
plucks up spirit, tries again and again, and in
the end very likely " wins out."

Just two or three examples. When the
wonderful violin prodigy, Franz von Vecsey,
over whom all Europe had raved, came to
New York in 1903, he was received with such
a volley of scathing criticism (and in one or
two cases of vituperative abuse), that his
manager, Mr. Daniel Frohman, was compelled
to cancel most of his tour and thereby incur
a heavy financial loss.

When Miss Geraldine Farrar made her
début at the Metropolitan Opera House, after
several brilliant seasons at Berlin, almost every
kind of fault was found with her. Like a true
American, she refused to be discouraged and
only went on working the harder. By degrees
she wore down her opposition and incidentally

corrected her real faults, becoming every year a finer artist. She is now an established favourite.

When Madame Tetrazzini first came to the Manhattan, just a year after she had created her extraordinary furore in London, her reception by the press was as cool as that of the public was replete with enthusiasm. Things were said about her vocalization that would have crushed an ordinary prima donna. But Madame Tetrazzini is not an ordinary prima donna. At this moment there is no more popular singer in America; while the critics of Philadelphia, Boston, and Baltimore, who praised her to the skies from the outset, confirmed the verdict of the London and New York public without an equivocal word.

But the effect of the sting is not unfelt or forgotten even by artists of this calibre. It rankles for a long while.

Take, for instance, Miss Mary Garden, whose phenomenal success was achieved in spite of the fiercest adverse criticism ever levelled at an American opera singer. Admitting that Miss Garden's vocal art left every

possible loophole for the shafts which she
encountered, one could not help admiring the
courage, nay, the audacity, with which she
flung back taunt for taunt and laughed openly
at her critics' lack of artistic perception. Her
blows may have been a trifle lacking in
discrimination, but she certainly had her
revenge.

Her anxiety on the night of her *début* in
"Thaïs" reminded one somewhat of Alvary's
at Covent Garden. After the second act I
went on the stage just as the fair Alexandrian
courtesan was tripping across in her diaphanous
blue robe for the scene at the Desert wells.
I congratulated her on her cordial reception,
and mentioned that I had just been chatting
with one of her sternest critics. She asked
me eagerly what he had said. "He told me,"
I replied, "that he was much struck by your
interesting personality."

Curiously enough, the critic in question
afterwards clung so tenaciously to his con-
cept that he scarcely ever referred to Miss
Garden without speaking of her "interesting

K

personality." Somehow I fancy she never forgot the circumstance.

From the illustrations just given one eloquent fact will be gathered—that the New York public does not invariably accept or endorse the opinions of its musical critics. As in the case of a new play, it occasionally takes the bit between its teeth and crowds the theatre without regard for what the papers have said. When this happens it is either because the attraction is in the nature of a sensation, or because the public has contrived to perceive therein certain merits that have escaped the observation of the critics.

What is the precise measure of the influence wielded by these musical chroniclers over their local readers ? I am not sure. Yet I would that I could answer the question definitely. For it is of importance as indicating how far the critics are responsible for the strange varieties of taste, the odd mixtures of fancy and caprice, which in New York seem to run the whole gamut of musical appreciation.

Of one thing, however, I am quite certain.

The critics, if they do not spare the artists, have a habit of flattering their readers that does undeniable harm. They declare with un-tiring reiteration that New York is the greatest musical city in the world ; that no other public can compare with it either for its love of Opera or the amount of money that it spends on Opera ; that its verdict is essential to the immortal fame of every star in the musical firmament ; that its opinions now stand higher in universal estimation than those of the leading European centres ; and so on, *ad nauseam.*

If this were all true there would still be cause for regret in a practice which fosters instead of tempering the self-satisfaction of a public already too prone to vanity and conceit. The duty of the critic is not only to criticize, but to inform and instruct and point out the right way.

As it is, the hard knocks are exclusively bestowed upon the individual who most needs courteous consideration, be that individual native or foreign—composer, conductor, execu-tant or singer.

As it is, between the lines of a New York notice may be too often read the underlying sentiment which says "What do you want here? We could do very well without you. What care we for your European successes and notices? We do not trust them. People over there are too quickly pleased. This public is not so easily satisfied. Ours is a higher standard. There are some things that we understand much better. It is impossible to hoodwink us. We are accustomed to hearing the world's greatest stars and most colossal masterpieces."

Indulgence towards the *débutant* is regarded as a sin. It is the exception, not the rule, to encourage rising talent by the simple expedient of laying stress upon good qualities, then pointing out defects and suggesting the way to correct them. This would be too gentle, too tolerant. On the other hand, much space is often wasted (not by the critic, perhaps, but by the newspaper) upon the studio performances of young people who are still in a state of tutelage. These lucubrations are not, however, so much for the benefit of the pupil as of the professor, who pays liberally for them through the medium of the advertising columns.

Anonymity has long ceased to be a wonted feature of musical journalism. Most of the New York critics sign their articles either with their names or their initials, and they are familiar figures in the world of music. It would be no serious breach of etiquette, therefore, to speak of them by name; but as there is no real need for this, I prefer to take a course less open to the charge of invidiousness.

Taken *en bloc* they are clever men and able journalists, not less fully equipped for their vocation than the critics of most big cities. Some may be better writers or more thorough musicians than others: but all are adroit masters of the phraseology of their profession and may be read with interest if not always with profit.

The New York critic is exceedingly frank. He does not stop to weigh the effect of his words upon the sensitive artistic cuticle. He deems it his business to be candid and plain-spoken ; he is so even to the length of employing a Nasmyth hammer to crack a nut—sometimes permanently injuring the kernel in the process. There are too many moments when he forgets that the pen is mightier than the sword.

But there is something he never does forget, and that is to impress the reader with a sense of his own absolute authority, of his own profound wisdom. Both qualities may be unquestionable, and, when united to a wide experience of musical history, both ought to command respect. But they would do so just as forcibly if conveyed with an undertone of truer and more evident modesty. The manifestation of a writer's power should exhibit itself in the *effect* of his words, not in the words themselves.

" As you are strong be merciful," would be an appropriate apostrophe to address to the New York critic. The possession of power carries with it a corresponding responsibility as to the exercise of the quality for which Portia pleaded.

A famous mid-Victorian novelist, Anthony

Trollope, put these words into the mouth of one of his finest characters—

"It is easy to condemn. I know no life that must be so delicious as that of a writer for the newspapers, or a leading member of the opposition—to thunder forth accusations against men in power ; show up the worst side in everything that is produced ; to pick holes in every coat ; to be indignant, sarcastic, jocose, moral, or supercilious ; to damn with faint praise, or crush with open calumny ! What can be so easy as this when the critic has to be responsible for nothing ? "

But in reality the critic who is worthy of the name cannot be "responsible for nothing." His is in truth a very serious responsibility.

The New York critic is hardly to be blamed for dealing largely in personalities. They are the life and soul of latter-day journalism. And yet if he needs must gratify the insatiable appetite of his readers in this direction, the stronger becomes the argument for his refraining from the kind of Chauvinistic flattery to which I have previously alluded. He is wrong, moreover, to pander to their weaknesses by praising the poor stuff that the masses love to listen to. Even when treading this lower level, it is his duty at all hazards to make the improvement of the public taste his chief consideration.

This should be the easier for him because I believe that at heart he really desires to encourage the best that his art can yield. The only drawback in the matter is the peculiar trend of his *penchants* and his prejudices.

He does not—for a critic—eliminate sufficiently his personal likes and dislikes. He loves to harp upon his favourite string and promote his particular fancy. He would see the composer of his choice represented in every programme ; he will belittle other composers to glorify that one. And, when it comes to singers, I am afraid he will not hesitate to laud his or New York's especial idol at the expense of a dozen vocal deities whom he has placed upon a lower pedestal. He does it neatly—perhaps unconsciously ; but he does it none the less.

To ask a critic to be entirely free from prejudice of every sort is akin to asking the same thing of a judge on the bench. It is the ideal condition ; but to err is human, and critics, like judges, are only human after all. If a wrong be done, the sole hope of righting it lies in an appeal to the supreme court of the people ; and that is not always easy of accomplishment.

One other trouble (it is the last I shall specify) that has its subtle influence upon musical criticism in New York is the fact that its exponents are becoming exceedingly *blasés*. They are not old men—far be it from me to even insinuate as much. On the contrary, take them individually, look at them, listen to them, and they still appear wonderfully young.

But, alas ! when it comes to writing, most of the fire and enthusiasm of youth, its freshness of sympathetic feeling, its faculty for appreciation and enjoyment, would seem to have abated. Their tone, their style of expression, betrays to the expert reader the sense of " weariness of the flesh " which, could it voice itself, would exclaim, " May there soon be less music in this world and none at all in the next ! "

Indeed, it is only fair to state that these gentlemen are now sadly overworked. They get a longer summer vacation than their European *confrères*, but they write on the average nearly double as much. Their Sunday articles are of portentous length, their over-night criticisms extend to columns, and they notice every change of cast, important or otherwise, in the operatic representations. On the principal daily papers, truly, they are now granted paid assistants, as is the case in London ; but unfortunately the reports of these deputies are quite colourless and of no real value except to " cover the event." * There is room for further and useful reform here.

* Payment for an advertisement in New York carries with it the prescriptive right to a notice in the editorial columns, though, of course, it cannot compel the attendance of the recognized critic of the paper. Still less can it influence the opinions of that critic. An operatic manager has been known to withdraw his advertisements because he objected to the unfriendly tone of the notices. Mr. Hammerstein has done this in two conspicuous instances. But the effect of the proceeding is not

And now I have done. Greatly daring, I have criticized the critics; and I have tried above all things to be just, to "Nothing extenuate, nor set down aught in malice." Therein rests my sole right to speak, my sole vindication, my sole claim to protection against the possible storm.

Whatever the methods of the New York critics I must not deny admiration to their exceptional literary gifts, their felicity of expression, their resourceful command of the English language, their talent for technical analysis.

But I have never believed in what is termed "destructive criticism," and of that particular sin these able writers cannot be held guiltless. They have no right to give their pens free licence and indulge the sheer enjoyment of inflicting pain upon the musicians whom they "vivisect." Instead of this, they should be ready and glad to help along the artist or composer who is struggling (and often deserves) to win "the bubble reputation."

pleasant, neither is it always efficacious, and the average person would not be well advised to try it.

I wish most heartily that they would be truer to themselves—thereby being truer to their readers—and not allow their views to be warped by prejudice. I wish they would manifest less of the *parti pris* and a little more of the "milk of human kindness."

Their power for good might be that of a vast concentrated force, working night and day like some huge machine which never stops. Would that it were only thus employed!

It is for the Press of New York, then, to complete the task which should be its dearest ambition—the task of raising its superb city to the level of the greatest musical centre in the world.

ENVOI

A NEW YORK reviewer, writing in 1903, applied to my book, "Thirty Years of Musical Life in London," the epithet "saponaceous." I suppose he meant, politely speaking, that the celebrities who figured therein had been treated with excessive consideration, that I had enlarged too liberally upon their merits and not accorded sufficient prominence to their faults and shortcomings. Well, he is not likely to say the same of this volume.

During the intervening years I have dwelt in the city of New York, where musical writers quickly acquire a habit of expressing themselves in austere, not to say morose fashion. Still I hope I have not swung from the "saponaceous" to that extreme. I would rather be accused of erring in the direction of indulgence than of undue harshness and rigour.

If I have been merely severe I am satisfied ; because those who are apt to be severe themselves ought not, if they are fair, to complain of the same tendency in others.

Anyhow, I have done my best to hold the scales evenly. As an Englishman writing, first, for the information of his countrymen, and, secondly, for the benefit of America's largest city, I have never for a moment lost sight of the familiar adage which alludes to "glass houses" and "stones."

But I take the risk because good may come of it. Nay, more, I again frankly confess my belief that the majority of New York's musical "failures and abuses" may be found rampant in a greater or lesser degree in the British metropolis.

If this be so, there is an Augean stable to be cleaned out on both sides of the Atlantic. Far be it from me, though, to aspire to the *rôle* of Ercles in either case. A humble observer of musical doings in two hemispheres may be permitted to point out the line of duty; he should not attempt feats that a mythological hero alone could perform single-handed.

After this candid acknowledgment pray let us hear naught from the other side of "British jealousy and prejudice." The present writer does not harbour such sentiments; neither does he believe in their survival *vis-à-vis* of that great country, the United States of America. He knows of them only as a fable, which he saw in print more frequently during his eight years in New York than he heard or read in England of Yankee misdeeds from the time the Alabama Claim was started.

As a member of "The Pilgrims," I am pledged, of my own free will, to support a society whose object is to knit together by every means in its power the ties that now unite Britons and Americans in closest friend-ship.

I trust that so long as I shall live no act of mine will be interpreted as having any other intent. Still less that this unbiassed criticism of a peculiar phase of American musical life shall be perused in any save the purely eclectic spirit in which I have striven to indite it.

FINIS